ACCA

PAPER F4

CORPORATE AND BUSINESS LAW (ENG)

BPP Learning Media is an **ACCA Approved Learning Partner – content** for the ACCA qualification. This means we work closely with ACCA to ensure our products fully prepare you for your ACCA exams.

In this Practice and Revision Kit, which has been reviewed by the **ACCA examination team,** we:

- Ensure you are well **prepared** for your exam

- Provide you with **lots of great guidance** on tackling questions

- Provide you with **three** mock exams

Our **Passcard** and **i-pass** products also support this paper.

FOR EXAMS UP TO JUNE 2015

BPP
LEARNING MEDIA

First edition 2008

Eighth edition June 2014

ISBN 9781 4727 1100 7
(previous ISBN 9781 4453 7992 0)

e-ISBN 9781 4727 1164 9

British Library Cataloguing-in-Publication Data
A catalogue record for this book
is available from the British Library

Published by

BPP Learning Media Ltd
BPP House, Aldine Place
London W12 8AA

www.bpp.com/learningmedia

Printed in the United Kingdom by Polestar Wheatons
Hennock Road
Marsh Barton
Exeter
EX2 8RP

o 00016069

We are grateful to the Association of Chartered Certified
Accountants for permission to reproduce past
examination questions. The suggested solutions have
been prepared by BPP Learning Media Ltd, except where
otherwise stated.

Your learning materials, published by BPP Learning
Media Ltd, are printed on paper obtained from
traceable, sustainable sources.

ii

Contents

A note about copyright

Dear Customer

What does the little © mean and why does it matter?

Your market-leading BPP books, course materials and e-learning materials do not write and update themselves. People write them: on their own behalf or as employees of an organisation that invests in this activity. Copyright law protects their livelihoods. It does so by creating rights over the use of the content.

Breach of copyright is a form of theft – as well as being a criminal offence in some jurisdictions, it is potentially a serious breach of professional ethics.

With current technology, things might seem a bit hazy but, basically, without the express permission of BPP Learning Media:

- Photocopying our materials is a breach of copyright

- Scanning, ripcasting or conversion of our digital materials into different file formats, uploading them to Facebook or emailing them to your friends is a breach of copyright

You can, of course, sell your books, in the form in which you have bought them – once you have finished with them. (Is this fair to your fellow students? We update for a reason.) Please note the e-products are sold on a single user licence basis: we do not supply 'unlock' codes to people who have bought them second-hand.

And what about outside the UK? BPP Learning Media strives to make our materials available at prices students can afford by local printing arrangements, pricing policies and partnerships which are clearly listed on our website. A tiny minority ignore this and indulge in criminal activity by illegally photocopying our material or supporting organisations that do. If they act illegally and unethically in one area, can you really trust them?

Question index

The headings in this checklist/index indicate the main topics of questions. Multiple Task Questions (MTQs) will cover material within the relevant part of the syllabus.

	Marks	Time allocation Mins	Page number Question	Page number Answer
Part F: Management, administration and regulation of companies				
22 Company directors	23	28	55	104
23 Other company officers	23	28	57	105
24 Company meetings and resolutions	23	28	59	106
25 MTQ Bank 5	30	36	61	107
Part G: Legal implications of companies in difficulty or in crisis				
26 Insolvency and administration	23	28	63	109
27 MTQ Bank 6	30	36	66	110
Part H: Governance and ethical issues relating to business				
28 Fraudulent and criminal behaviour	23	28	68	112
29 MTQ Bank 7	30	36	71	113
Mock Exams				
Mock Exam 1	100	120	119	129
Mock Exam 2	100	120	137	149
Mock Exam 3 (Specimen Paper)	100	120	157	169

Helping you with your revision

Making the most of question practice

At BPP Learning Media we realise that you need more than just questions and model answers to get the most from your question practice.

- Our **top tips** included for certain questions provide essential advice on tackling questions, presenting answers and the key points that answers need to include.

- At the end of this Kit we include the **official ACCA answers** to the Specimen paper.

Attempting mock exams

There are three mock exams that provide practice at coping with the pressures of the exam day. We strongly recommend that you attempt them under exam conditions. **Mock exams 1 and 2** reflect the question styles and syllabus coverage of the exam; **Mock exam 3** is the Specimen paper.

Revising F4

Topics to revise

All questions are compulsory so you must revise the **whole** syllabus. Since the exam includes 45 multiple choice questions in Section A, you should expect questions to cover a large part of the syllabus. Selective revision **will limit** the number of questions you can answer and hence reduce your chances of passing. It is better to go into the exam knowing a reasonable amount about most of the syllabus rather than concentrating on a few topics to the exclusion of the rest.

Question practice

Practising as many exam-style questions as possible will be the key to passing this exam. You must do questions under **timed conditions**.

Avoid looking at the answers until you have finished a question bank. Your biggest problem with the MTQ questions may be knowing how to start, and this needs practice.

Also ensure that you attempt all three mock exams under exam conditions.

Passing the F4 exam

Displaying the right qualities

- You will be required to identify the requirements of multiple choice questions quickly, so that you can make your answers confidently within the available time

- You will be required to interpret scenarios and apply your knowledge to them

- You must therefore be able to apply your skills in a practical context

Avoiding weaknesses

- There is no choice in this paper, all questions have to be answered. You must therefore study the entire syllabus, there are no short-cuts.

- The ability to answer multiple choice questions improves with practice. Try to get as much practice with these questions as you can.

- The multiple task questions (MTQs) will be based on simple scenarios and answers must be focused and specific to the situation.

- Attempt all parts of the MTQs. Even if you cannot answer them in full, you can still gain some marks.

Gaining the easy marks

Easy marks in this paper fall into two categories.

Multiple choice questions (MCQs)

Some MCQs are easier than others and will take less time to process. Answer those that you feel fairly confident about as quickly as you can. Come back later to those you find more difficult. This could be a way of making use of the time in the examination most efficiently and effectively.

Multiple task questions (MTQs)

Many questions will have some element of knowledge that you can answer quickly, so focus on these sub-parts first. Most of the marks, however, will be available for applying your knowledge to the scenario. Read the question carefully and more than once, to ensure you are actually answering the specific requirements.

Keep your answers as short as possible. As an indication, a two-mark part is likely to be answerable in no more than a few sentences. Clearly label the points you make so that the marker can identify them all rather than getting lost in the detail.

The Computer Based Examination

Computer based examinations (CBEs) are available for the English and Global variants of the F4 exam in addition to the conventional paper based examination.

Computer based examinations must be taken at an ACCA CBE Licensed Centre.

How does CBE work?

- Questions are displayed on a monitor

- Candidates enter their answer directly onto the computer

- Candidates have two hours to complete the examination

- When the candidate has completed their examination, the final percentage score is calculated and displayed on screen

- Candidates are provided with a Provisional Result Notification showing their results before leaving the examination room

- The CBE Licensed Centre uploads the results to the ACCA (as proof of the candidate's performance) within 72 hours

- Candidates can check their exam status on the ACCA website by logging into myACCA.

Benefits

- **Flexibility** as a CBE can be sat at any time.

- **Resits** can also be taken at any time and there is no restriction on the number of times a candidate can sit a CBE.

- **Instant feedback** as the computer displays the results at the end of the CBE.

- Results are notified to ACCA **within 72 hours**.

CBE question types

- Multiple choice – choose one answer from three or four options

- Multiple response – select one or more responses by clicking the appropriate tick boxes

- Multiple response matching – select a response to a number of related part questions by choosing one option from a selection

The **BPP Learning Media i-pass** product provides exam practice for students intending to take the computer based exam.

Tackling Multiple Choice Questions

The MCQs in your exam contain three or four possible answers. You have to **choose the option that best answers the question**. The incorrect options are called distracters. There is a skill in answering MCQs quickly and correctly. By practising MCQs you can develop this skill, giving you a better chance of passing the exam.

You may wish to follow the approach outlined below, or you may prefer to adapt it.

Step 1	Skim read all the MCQs and identify what appear to be the easier questions.
Step 2	Attempt each question – **starting with the easier questions** identified in Step 1. Read the question **thoroughly**. You may prefer to work out the answer before looking at the options, or you may prefer to look at the options at the beginning. Adopt the method that works best for you.
Step 3	Read the four options and see if one matches your own answer.
Step 4	You may find that none of the options matches your answer. • Re-read the question to ensure that you understand it and are answering the requirement • Eliminate any obviously wrong answers • Consider which of the remaining answers is the most likely to be correct and select the option
Step 5	If you are still unsure make a note and continue to the next question
Step 6	Revisit unanswered questions. When you come back to a question after a break you often find you are able to answer it correctly straight away. If you are still unsure have a guess. You are not penalised for incorrect answers, so **never leave a question unanswered!**

After extensive practice and revision of MCQs, you may find that you recognise a question when you sit the exam. Be aware that the detail and/or requirement may be different. If the question seems familiar read the requirement and options carefully – do not assume that it is identical.

Exam information

Format of the exam

All questions are compulsory.

45 multiple choice questions in Section A, each worth 1 or 2 marks. A total of 70 marks are available.

5 multiple task questions in Section B, each worth 6 marks. A total of 30 marks are available.

Time allowed: 2 hours

Additional information

The Study Guide provides more detailed guidance on the syllabus.

Useful websites

The websites below provide additional sources of information of relevance to your studies of *Corporate and Business Law.*

- www.accaglobal.com

  ACCA's website. The students' section of the website is invaluable for detailed information about the qualification, past issues of Student Accountant (including technical articles) and even interviews with the examiners.

- www.bpp.com

  Our website provides information about BPP products and services, with a link to the ACCA website.

- www.ft.com

  This website provides information about current international business. You can search for information and articles on specific industry groups as well as individual companies.

- www.iclr.co.uk

  The Incorporated Council of Law Reporting

- www.lawrights.co.uk

  Source of free legal information

- www.lawsociety.org.uk

  Law Society

- www.bbc.co.uk

  The website of the BBC carries general business information as well as programme-related content.

Questions

1 Law and the legal system

1.1 Which of the following is the prosecutor in a criminal law case?

    A   The State
    B   The accused
    C   The victim   **(1 mark)**

1.2 Which of the following describes the standard of proof in a civil law case?

    A   Beyond reasonable doubt
    B   Balance of probability
    C   Beyond all probability   **(1 mark)**

1.3 Which of the following is a remedy available under the civil law?

    A   A fine
    B   Imprisonment
    C   Damages   **(1 mark)**

1.4 All criminal law cases begin in which of the following courts?

    A   The County Court
    B   The Magistrate's Court
    C   The Crown Court   **(1 mark)**

1.5 The Queen's Bench, Family and Chancery are all division of which court?

    A   Crown Court
    B   Supreme Court
    C   High Court   **(1 mark)**

1.6 Which of the following statements concerning cases brought before a Magistrate's Courts is correct?

    A   The case is decided by the Magistrate rather than a jury
    B   Only criminal cases are heard at a Magistrate's Court
    C   Appeals are made directly to the Court of Appeal   **(1 mark)**

1.7 Which of the following offences would only be heard at a Magistrate's Court?

    A   An indictable offence
    B   A summary offence
    C   A 'triable either way' offence   **(1 mark)**

1.8 Which type of law is concerned with the function and operation of local authorities?

    A   Public Law
    B   Private Law
    C   Common Law
    D   Equity   **(2 marks)**

1.9 Which TWO of the following terms are associated with criminal law rather than civil law?

    (1)   Punishment
    (2)   Public law
    (3)   Compensation
    (4)   Claimant

    A   1 and 2
    B   1 and 4
    C   2 and 3
    D   3 and 4   **(2 marks)**

1.10 Which TWO of the following are the parties involved in a civil law case?

(1) Accused
(2) Defendant
(3) Claimant
(4) Prosecution

A 1 and 4
B 1 and 3
C 2 and 3
D 2 and 4 **(2 marks)**

1.11 In the civil law system, cases are allocated to one of three 'tracks' for processing.

Which of the following is NOT a 'track' in the civil law system?

A Fast
B Medium
C Small
D Multi **(2 marks)**

1.12 In the criminal law system, an immediate appeal regarding a decision by a Magistrate's Court could be heard by which of the following courts?

A The County Court
B The Crown Court
C The Court of Appeal
D The Supreme Court **(2 marks)**

1.13 Which of the following courts only has civil jurisdiction?

A The County Court
B The Magistrate's Court
C The Court of Appeal
D The Privy Council **(2 marks)**

1.14 The Chancery Division of the High Court hears cases involving which of the following matters?

A Contract law
B Trusts and mortgages
C Matrimonial cases
D Adoption of children **(2 marks)**

1.15 Which TWO of the following are types of offences heard by a Magistrate's Court?

(1) Indictable
(2) Summary
(3) Triable either way
(4) Hybrid

A 1 and 3
B 1 and 4
C 2 and 3
D 2 and 4 **(2 marks)**

(Total = 23 marks)

2 Sources of law

2.1 Which of the following is a statement by a judge that is the basis for their decision and is what becomes binding on future judges?

    A   Obiter dicta
    B   Per incuriam
    C   Ratio decidendi   **(1 mark)**

2.2 Which of the following types of court decision occurs when a court higher in the hierarchy overturns the verdict of a lower court in the same case?

    A   Reversing
    B   Overruling
    C   Distinguishing   **(1 mark)**

2.3 Which of the following statements in relation to legislation is correct?

    A   Legislation may modify or replace existing statutes
    B   Legislation may not overrule or modify existing case law
    C   Legislation may prevent a subsequent Parliament from changing the law   **(1 mark)**

2.4 Which of the following types of legislation affects specific individuals or groups?

    A   Enabling
    B   Public
    C   Private   **(1 mark)**

2.5 Which rule of statutory interpretation states that words in a statute should be given their plain, ordinary meaning unless this would give rise to a manifest absurdity or inconsistency with the rest of the statute?

    A   Golden rule
    B   Mischief rule
    C   Contextual rule   **(1 mark)**

2.6 Which of the following is an intrinsic aid to statutory interpretation?

    A   Hansard
    B   The long title of the Act
    C   Law commission reports   **(1 mark)**

2.7 Which of the following is the final appeal court for human rights issues for persons living in the UK?

    A   Supreme Court
    B   European Court of Human Rights
    C   European Court of Justice   **(1 mark)**

2.8 The decisions of which of the following courts is binding on the Court of Appeal?

    A   The County Court
    B   The Crown Court
    C   The High Court
    D   The Court of Appeal   **(2 marks)**

2.9 Which of the following statements concerning the principle of binding precedent is NOT correct?

    A   Mistakes by judges are eliminated
    B   General legal principles are established
    C   The law is based on actual, rather than theoretical, cases
    D   The law is flexible and can develop with changing circumstances   **(2 marks)**

2.10 Which TWO of the following are stages that a Bill passes through before becoming legislation?

(1) Report stage
(2) Committee stage
(3) Fourth reading
(4) Approval stage

A   1 and 2
B   1 and 3
C   2 and 3
D   2 and 4   **(2 marks)**

2.11 Some statutory instruments require a resolution of Parliament to come into effect, but others must be laid before Parliament for a particular period of time before coming in effect.

How many days must statutory instruments be laid before Parliament before coming into effect?

A   10
B   20
C   30
D   40   **(2 marks)**

2.12 Which rule or approach to statutory interpretation considers what the the legislation is trying to achieve?

A   Contextual rule
B   Literal rule
C   Purposive approach
D   Golden rule   **(2 marks)**

2.13 Presumptions of statutory interpretation provide judges with rules to use when interpreting legislation.

Which of the following statements in relation to the presumptions of statutory interpretation is correct?

A   A statute may not deprive a person of their property
B   A statute does not have retrospective effect
C   A statute binds the Crown
D   A statute has effect outside the UK   **(2 marks)**

2.14 Which of the following is an extrinsic aid to statutory interpretation?

A   Hansard
B   The long title of the Act
C   The preamble of the Act
D   Side notes to the statute   **(2 marks)**

2.15 Which TWO of the following statements in relation to the impact of the Human Rights Act 1998 on legislation are correct?

(1) All new primary legislation must be compatible with the European Convention on Human Rights
(2) The courts may strike out secondary legislation that is incompatible with the European Convention on Human Rights
(3) Courts must interpret legislation in such a way that is compatible with the European Convention on Human Rights
(4) Under the Human Rights Act 1998, courts are not required to take the decisions of the European Court of Justice when making their decisions

A   1 and 3
B   1 and 4
C   2 and 3
D   2 and 4   **(2 marks)**

(Total = 23 marks)

3 Formation of contract I

28 mins

3.1 Which of the following contracts must be in the form of a deed?

A   A conveyance (a transfer of a legal estate in land)
B   A transfer of shares
C   A consumer credit contract

(1 mark)

3.2 In relation to contract law, which of the following describes an offer?

A   A statement of possible terms
B   Displaying goods for sale in a supermarket
C   A verbal promise to be bound on specific terms

(1 mark)

3.3 In a sale by auction that is stated to be 'without reserve', at which point is an offer made?

A   When the auctioneer presents the goods being sold
B   When a bid is made
C   When the auctioneer's hammer falls

(1 mark)

3.4 In relation to contract law, how long will an offer remain open if no time period is set for its expiry?

A   1 day
B   1 month
C   For a reasonable time

(1 mark)

3.5 Which of the following will terminate an offer?

A   Posting a letter of revocation
B   A request for information
C   Death of the offeree

(1 mark)

3.6 Which of the following is NOT a valid method of acceptance?

A   The offeree's express words
B   The offeree's conduct
C   Silence of the offeree

(1 mark)

3.7 Which of the following statements regarding the postal rule is correct?

A   Acceptance is effective once the letter of acceptance is written
B   Acceptance is effective once the letter of acceptance is posted
C   Acceptance is effective once the letter of acceptance is delivered

(1 mark)

3.8 Which of the following is an example of a standard form contract?

A   A verbal agreement between two private individuals
B   A contract for the sale of a house between two private individuals
C   A contract for the supply of electricity between a utility company and a private individual
D   A contract of employment between a private individual and a small local shop

(2 marks)

3.9 Which of the following statements concerning the law and contracts is correct?

A   The law seeks to ensure equal bargaining power between parties
B   The law will only interfere in contracts where one party abuses a stronger bargaining position
C   The law does not interfere in the formation of contracts
D   The law seeks to maintain the bargaining power of parties in a contract

(2 marks)

3.10   Which TWO of the following are examples of valid offers?

   (1)   A person verbally stating to another person that they would like to sell their computer to them for
          £500 today
   (2)   A newspaper advert that states a shop is selling shoes for £20
   (3)   A person handing their shopping to a supermarket checkout operator
   (4)   A business that circulates its price list to customers

   A   1 and 2
   B   1 and 3
   C   2 and 3
   D   2 and 4   (2 marks)

3.11   Which of the following is an example of a valid offer?

   A   A display of goods for sale
   B   An Internet shop that advertises products for sale
   C   A newspaper advert that includes a specific statement, made to the world at large, offering a reward
        for the return of a particular item
   D   An invition for potential suppliers to tender for the provision of services   (2 marks)

3.12   Which of the following statements regarding counter-offers is correct?

   A   Counter-offers may be accepted by the original offeror
   B   Counter-offers do not terminate the original offer
   C   A statement that enquires whether alternative terms would be acceptable is a counter-offer
   D   A counter-offer is made by the original offeror to the original offeree   (2 marks)

3.13   In which of the following situations will an offer be terminated?

   A   When a letter of revocation is posted
   B   When a third party, who is sufficiently reliable, verbally notifies the offeror of the offeree's revocation
   C   When an offeree enquires whether the offeror will accept payment by credit card rather than cash
   D   When an offeror dies, the offeree is unaware of the death and the contract is not of a personal nature
                                                                                              (2 marks)

3.14   Which of the following would be regarded as valid, binding acceptance?

   A   A counter-offer
   B   Acceptance 'subject to contract'
   C   A tender to perform one task
   D   Posting a letter of acceptance   (2 marks)

3.15   Which TWO of the following statements regarding acceptance of an offer are correct?

   (1)   Acceptance does not need to be communicated in a unilateral contract
   (2)   If two identical offers between two parties cross in the post, then one will be regarded as acceptance
          of the other
   (3)   Under the postal rule, a letter of acceptance that has been posted does not have to be receieved by
          the offeror to be valid acceptance
   (4)   If no method of communicating acceptance is stated in the offer, then acceptance must be made by
          post

   A   1 and 2
   B   1 and 3
   C   2 and 3
   D   2 and 4   (2 marks)

                                                                                    (Total = 23 marks)

4 Formation of contract II

4.1 Which of the following is executed consideration?

A   Providing goods in return for payment at the same time
B   A promise of payment in return for the provision of goods at a later date
C   A promise to pay for work already carried out   **(1 mark)**

4.2 Which of the following describes how courts deal with the adequacy of consideration?

A   Courts will seek to ensure that consideration from each party is of equal value
B   Courts will seek to ensure no party makes excess profit
C   Courts will not interfere in a contract to rectify a bad bargain   **(1 mark)**

4.3 Which of the following statements regarding the adequacy and sufficiency of consideration is correct?

A   Consideration does not need to have a value to be sufficient
B   Consideration is sufficient if it has some economic value
C   Consideration does not need to be sufficient but must be adequate   **(1 mark)**

4.4 Which of the following is true regarding privity of contract?

A   Third parties to a contract generally have enforceable rights under it
B   Only parties to a contract generally have enforceable rights under it
C   Privity of contract only relates to rights under a contract, not obligations   **(1 mark)**

4.5 Which of the following is NOT an exception to the rule of privity of contract?

A   A third party to a contract can sue for losses they incur under a contract if the lossess are foreseeable
B   A third party to a contract can bring an action under it if an implied trust has been created
C   A third party to a contract can enforce rights under it if it is equitable for them to do so   **(1 mark)**

4.6 Which of the following statements regarding intention to create legal relations is correct?

A   Social arrangements are generally intended to be legally binding
B   Commercial arrangements are generally not intended to be legally binding
C   A contract will be legally binding if both parties intended it to be so   **(1 mark)**

4.7 Which of the following indicates that the parties intend to be legally bound?

A   A letter of comfort
B   An agreement between a husband and wife to transfer property between them
C   An agreement 'binding in honour only'   **(1 mark)**

4.8 Which of the following is a correct rule for valid consideration?

A   Consideration must pass from the promisee
B   Consideration must be adequate
C   Past consideration is generally valid consideration
D   Executory consideration is generally not valid consideration   **(2 marks)**

4.9 Which of the following statements is true of consideration?

A   Past consideration is sufficient to create liability on a bill of exchange
B   Suffering some loss or detriment is not valid consideration
C   Consideration can be in the form of any act, even if that act is impossible to perform
D   Performance of an illegal act is valid consideration   **(2 marks)**

4.10 Where a party accepts part payment for a debt, they may at a later date request payment of the amount outstanding unless the other party provided extra consideration when making the part payment.

Which TWO of the following are valid extra consideration for part payment of a debt?

(1) Payment in the form of goods rather than cash
(2) Payment by a third party rather than the debtor
(3) An intention by the debtor to be legally bound by the part payment
(4) A guarantee by the debtor to make the payment on the date agreed in the contract

A   1 and 2
B   1 and 4
C   2 and 3
D   2 and 4   (2 marks)

4.11 Which of the following statements regarding consideration is correct?

A   Performance of an existing legal obligation is valid consideration for the promise of additional reward
B   Performance of an existing contractual duty is sufficient consideration for the promise of additional reward
C   Performance of an existing contractual duty to a third party is sufficient consideration for the promise of additional reward
D   Performance of an extra service in addition to an existing contractual duty is not sufficient consideration for the promise of additional reward   (2 marks)

4.12 Which of the following statements concerning privity of contract is correct?

A   Privity of contract means only parties to a contract may sue on it
B   Privity of contract is not subject to regulation by statute
C   There are no exceptions to the rule of privity of contract
D   Privity of contract is only enforceable on commercial contracts   (2 marks)

4.13 The Contracts (Rights of Third Parties) Act 1999 sets out the circumstances where a third party has a right to enforce rights they may have under a contract.

Which of the following statements concerning the Contracts (Rights of Third Parties) Act 1999 is correct?

A   The third party need not be expressly identified in the contract
B   The third party need not be in existence when the contract was formed
C   The Act confers rights to third parties under a company's constitution
D   The Act confers rights to third parties under employment contracts   (2 marks)

4.14 Which of the following is true regarding presumptions of intention to create legal relations?

A   Parties in social, domestic and family agreements never intend to be legally bound
B   Parties in commercial agreements never intend to be legally bound
C   The presumption in all agreements is that the parties intend to be legally bound
D   Any presumptions in regards to the intention of parties to be legally bound may be refuted and the burden of proof is on the party seeking to escape liability   (2 marks)

4.15 Which TWO of the following social, domestic and family contracts would be presumed by the courts as intended to be legally binding?

(1) An agreement where a father offers to pay his daughter a monthly allowance if she continues her education

(2) An agreement between friends to enter a newspaper competition together and share any prizes between them

(3) An agreement between a husband and wife who have separated for one to rent the family home from the other

(4) An agreement by a son to pay his mother housekeeping money while he stays at home

A 1 and 3
B 1 and 4
C 2 and 3
D 2 and 4

(2 marks)

(Total = 23 marks)

5 Content of contracts

5.1 Which of the following actions can a party take where a term of a contract proves untrue?

A   Sue for breach of contract
B   Sue for misrepresentation
C   Sue for wrongful contract   **(1 mark)**

5.2 Which of the following statements is true regarding representations?

A   A representation is not a term of a contract
B   A representation does not induce the formation of a contract
C   A representation is a statement made after a contract was formed   **(1 mark)**

5.3 Which of the following statements regarding implied terms is correct?

A   Terms may be implied into a contract by statute
B   The courts do not interfere in contracts by implying terms
C   Terms implied into contracts by custom may not be overridden by express terms to the contrary   **(1 mark)**

5.4 In relation to contract law, which of the following describes a warranty?

A   A term vital to the contract, that if breached, entitles the injured party to treat the contract as discharged
B   A term subsidiary to the main purpose of the contract, that if breached, entitles the injured party to claim damages
C   A term that is not expressly stated by the parties   **(1 mark)**

5.5 Which of the following is true concerning the incorporation of terms into contracts?

A   A person is not bound by a contract they have signed if they have not read it
B   A history of consistent dealings between the parties is not sufficient to incorporate terms into a contract
C   Particularly unusual or onerous terms in a contract must be sufficiently highlighted   **(1 mark)**

5.6 In relation to exclusion clauses, which of the following describes the contra proferentem rule?

A   Exclusion clauses are valid unless unreasonable
B   Any ambiguity in exclusion clauses are interpreted against the person seeking to rely on them
C   Exclusion clauses must be validly incorporated into the contract   **(1 mark)**

5.7 In relation to exclusion clauses, which of the following describes the main purpose rule?

A   The purpose of an exclusion clause is not to prevent the main purpose of the contract
B   The main purpose of an exclusion clause is to help a weaker party avoid unfair contractual obligations
C   The main purpose of an exclusion clause is to give business efficacy to a contract   **(1 mark)**

5.8 At which point in a contractual arrangement is a representation made?

A   When the offeree submits their acceptance to the offeror
B   During pre-contract negotiations
C   When the offeror submits their offer to the offeree
D   Once both parties have provided consideration under their agreement   **(2 marks)**

5.9   How are express terms incorporated into a contract?

A   By a decision of the courts
B   By statute law
C   By the parties themselves
D   By what is customary in the particular trade   **(2 marks)**

5.10   Which TWO of the following statements regarding contractual terms are correct?

(1)   The principle of freedom of contract states that parties may include in their contract any terms that they see fit
(2)   To be valid, a contract must be complete in its terms
(3)   Third parties may not determine an essential term of the contract
(4)   Where a term is classified as a condition, the only remedy to an injured party if it is breached is to claim damages

A   1 and 2
B   1 and 4
C   2 and 3
D   2 and 4   **(2 marks)**

5.11   An innominate term is one that could either be classified as a condition or a warranty.

How is the classification of an innominate term as a condition or a warranty determined?

A   By the operation of statute law
B   By the offeror
C   By the courts
D   By the offeree   **(2 marks)**

5.12   Which of the following statements concerning exclusion clauses is correct?

A   Exclusion clauses can be incorporated into a contract after the contract is formed
B   Exclusion clauses are interpreted by the courts strictly
C   Exclusion clauses are not regulated by statute
D   Exclusion clauses may not exclude liability for negligence   **(2 marks)**

5.13   Which of the following exclusion clauses is void under the Unfair Contract Terms Act 1977?

A   A guarantee clause that limits loss or damage caused by a defect in a consumer good
B   A clause in a commercial contract that excludes liability for loss of profit due to negligence
C   A clause in a commercial contract that excludes liability for breach of contract
D   Any exclusion clause in a contract of insurance   **(2 marks)**

5.14   Which of the following statements concerning the Unfair Terms in Consumer Contracts Regulations 1999 is correct?

A   The regulations only apply to consumer contracts
B   The regulations only apply to terms that have been individually negotiated
C   The regulations allow a company to be classed as a consumer
D   The regulations allow a natural person who is acting in the course of their business to be classed as a consumer   **(2 marks)**

5.15 Which of the following statements concerning the Unfair Contract Terms Act 1977 is correct?

A   The Act only applies to consumer contracts
B   The Act does not apply to terms that have been individually negotiated
C   The Act allows a company to be classed as a consumer
D   The Act automatically voids all clauses that restrict liability for loss or damage due to negligence

(2 marks)

(Total = 23 marks)

6 Breach of contract and remedies
28 mins

6.1 Which of the following statements is NOT a lawful excuse for failing to perform contractual obligations?

   A   Actual performance is impossible
   B   Both parties agreed to non-performace
   C   Performing the contract will cause the party concerned financial hardship   **(1 mark)**

6.2 At which point does anticipatory breach of contract occur?

   A   At the time performance is due
   B   Before the time performance is due
   C   After the time performance is due   **(1 mark)**

6.3 Which of the following correctly describes the type of repudiatory breach known as renunciation?

   A   One party states that they have no intention to perform their obligations
   B   One party prevents themselves from performing their obligations
   C   One party is prevented from performing their obligations by external circumstances   **(1 mark)**

6.4 In relation to the award of damages in contract law, which of the following describes damages paid to protect the claimant's reliance interest?

   A   What is needed to put the claimant into the position they would have been in if the contract had been performed
   B   What is needed to put the claimant into the position they would have been in if they had not relied on the contract
   C   What is needed to recover the price of goods or services provided under the contract   **(1 mark)**

6.5 In relation to contract law, which of the following describes liquidated damages?

   A   A genuine pre-estimate of losses payable in the event of breach of contract
   B   A specific sum payable in the event of a breach of contract to punish a party for their breach
   C   A sum equal to the amount of work done plus an element of profit that is payable in the event of a breach of contract   **(1 mark)**

6.6 In which of the following circumstances would an award of specific performance be made?

   A   In breach of contract in an employment contract
   B   In breach of contract in a contract for personal services
   C   In breach of contract in a contract involving the sale of property   **(1 mark)**

6.7 Which of the following is an example of an equitable remedy for breach of contract?

   A   Injunction
   B   Action for the price
   C   Quantum meruit   **(1 mark)**

6.8 Which of the following is true concerning the rights of an innocent party where repudiatory breach of contract has occurred?

   A   If the innocent party chooses to terminate the contract they are not required to notify the other party
   B   The innocent party can claim damages for any losses but not treat the contract as discharged
   C   The innocent party cannot refuse to pay for partial or defective performance already receieved
   D   The innocent party may affirm the contract and continue with their obligations   **(2 marks)**

6.9 Which of the following is NOT a lawful excuse for failing to perform contractual obligations?

A   Performance is rejected by the other party
B   Performance is made impossible by the other party
C   Performance is rendered more expensive than agreed due to external circumstances
D   Non-performance was agreed between the parties   **(2 marks)**

6.10 Which TWO of the following are tests that should be met when determining whether damages are too remote to be claimed?

(1)   Losses must be connected in some way to the breach of contract
(2)   Losses must arise naturally from the breach of contract
(3)   Losses related to exceptional circumstances are too remote to be claimed
(4)   Losses arising outside the normal course of events will be compensated if the circumstances are within the defendant's knowledge when they formed to contract

A   1 and 4
B   1 and 3
C   2 and 3
D   2 and 4   **(2 marks)**

6.11 In relation to the law of contract, which of the following statements in relation to damages is correct?

A   Damages are not payable in relation to mental distress
B   Damages to rectify a defect are still payable even if they are wholly disproportionate to the size of the breach
C   An innocent party is required to take reasonable steps to mitigate their losses
D   Damages in the form of a penalty clause are valid and enforceable   **(2 marks)**

6.12 Which of the following statements in relation to liquidated damages is correct?

A   Liquidated damage clauses are void and unenforceable in contract law
B   Liquidated damage clauses must be highlighted in the contract
C   The purpose of liquidated damage clauses is to deter potential breaches of contract
D   Liquidated damages are only payable where a condition of a contract is breached   **(2 marks)**

6.13 Which of the following is true regarding injunctions?

A   Injunctions are a common law remedy
B   A court has no discretion as to whether or not to award an injunction
C   Injunctions require a defendant to observe a negative restriction of a contract
D   Injunctions may be awarded in conjunction with an award for damages   **(2 marks)**

6.14 Rescission is an equitable remedy, and where available, makes the contract voidable. There are a number of conditions attached to the award of rescission.

Which of the following is a condition that must be met for an award of rescission to be made?

A   The innocent party, only, must be able to be restored to their pre-contract position
B   The right to rescind the contract must be exercised within 30 days of it being awarded
C   Rescission must take place after the contract is affirmed
D   Innocent third parties must not have acquired rights under the subject matter of the contract   **(2 marks)**

6.15 For an order for specific performance to be made, which TWO of the following criteria must be met?

(1) Damages must be inadequate compensation
(2) Consideration must have passed between the parties
(3) The parties must both agree to the award
(4) The contract must require performance over a long period of time

A 1 and 2
B 1 and 3
C 2 and 3
D 2 and 4

(2 marks)

(Total = 23 marks)

7 The law of torts and professional negligence

28 mins

7.1 Which of the following statements concerning tort is correct?

    A   Breach of contract is a tort

    B   Torts are crimes

    C   A tort is a civil wrong and the victim sues for compensation or an injunction   **(1 mark)**

7.2 Which of the following describes the tort of 'passing-off'?

    A   The use of a business name or trademark that misleads the consumer to believe that one business is that of another

    B   Misleading a consumer to take actions that are to their detriment

    C   A consumer deliberately wearing a product that purports to be made by one brand but which is actually a fake   **(1 mark)**

7.3 In which of the following circumstances will a defendant be liable to pay compensation under the tort of negligence?

    A   They breached a duty of care to the claimant

    B   They breached a duty of care to the claimant and as a consequence the claimant suffered loss, injury or damage

    C   Their actions caused the claimant to suffer some loss, injury or damage   **(1 mark)**

7.4 In the tort of negligence, what is the legal effect of res ipsa loquitur?

    A   The claimant must prove that the defendant was negligent

    B   The defendant must prove that they were not negligent

    C   The claimant must prove that they acted reasonably   **(1 mark)**

7.5 In the tort of negligence, which type of loss is usually not recoverable?

    A   Pure economic loss

    B   Injury

    C   Damage to property   **(1 mark)**

7.6 In the tort of negligence, what is the effect of volenti non fit injuria?

    A   The defendant is liable for the claimant's injury unless proved otherwise

    B   The claimant accepted the risk of injury and the defendant is not liable for the claimant's losses

    C   Neither the claimant nor the defendant is responsible for the claimant's injury   **(1 mark)**

7.7 Which of the following statements describes whom an company's auditor owes a duty of care to?

    A   The public at large who read the company accounts

    B   The company's shareholders who increase their stake in the business

    C   The company only   **(1 mark)**

7.8 Which of the following statements regarding tort is correct?

    A   The only remedy for a victim of a tort is damages

    B   No contractual relationship need exist between claimant and defendant for the defendant to be liable to the claimant in tort

    C   Actions in tort are heard in the criminal court system

    D   In tort, the burden of proof is always on the defendant to prove that they were not negligent   **(2 marks)**

7.9 To establish a case of 'passing-off', what must the claimant prove?

    A   The consumer purchased fake goods
    B   The defendant is using a similar business model to the claimant
    C   The name of the defendant's business is similar enough to the claimant's to mislead the consumer
    D   There is some similarity between the name of the defendant's business and that of the claimant

(2 marks)

7.10 Which TWO of the following are questions that are asked to established whether the defendant owed the claimant a duty of care?

    (1)   Was the harm obvious to a reasonable person?
    (2)   Was there a relationship of proximity between the parties?
    (3)   Did the claimant accept the risk of injury?
    (4)   Is it fair, just and reasonable to impose a duty of care on the defendant?

    A   1 and 2
    B   1 and 3
    C   2 and 3
    D   2 and 4

(2 marks)

7.11 When considering whether a defendant has breached their duty of care, a number of factors are considered.

Which of the following statements concerning breach of duty of care is correct?

    A   Where there is a high probability of injury, the claimant should have taken extra care
    B   A social benefit to a defendant's actions is no excuse for breaching the level of care expected
    C   Defendants are not expected to ensure that all possible precautions against risk are taken if the cost of the precautions outweigh the risk
    D   A professional is expected to demonstrate the same level of care and skill as a reasonable person performing the same task

(2 marks)

7.12 Which of the following circumstances will prevent causality being established in a claim of negligence?

    A   An act of the claimant that is unreasonable and outside the normal course of things
    B   Acts of a third party that occur after the claimant's injury
    C   Foreseeable natural events
    D   Multiple possible reasons for the injury with no one act being established as the cause   **(2 marks)**

7.13 In a negligence case, the amount of compensation due to the claimant can be reduced if it is established that they contributed to their injury or loss.

What is the maximum reduction the courts will allow in cases of contributory negligence?

    A   25%
    B   50%
    C   75%
    D   100%   **(2 marks)**

7.14 Which of the following statements concerning the duty of care of accountants involved in preparing a report for a target company involved in a take-over bid is correct?

    A   The accountants owe a duty of care to the bidding company
    B   The accountants owe a higher standard of care to the target company than it would when auditing
    C   The accountants owe a duty of care to shareholders considering purchasing shares in the bidding company
    D   The accountants owe a duty of care to the general public considering purchasing shares in the target company

(2 marks)

7.15 Which TWO of the following parties does an auditor owe a duty of care to when auditing the accounts of a subsidiary company?

(1) The parent company
(2) The shareholders of the parent company
(3) The subsidiary company
(4) A rival company considering a takeover of the subsidiary company

A 1 and 2
B 1 and 3
C 2 and 3
D 2 and 4

(2 marks)

(Total = 23 marks)

8.1   On Friday 10 December the following notice is placed in the window of Ann's art gallery: '2 copies of a very rare Blake print – £15,000 each'. Chas and Dave are very keen to acquire the prints but think that the price is too high. They each offer Ann £12,000 for a copy but she refuses to sell the prints at that price, although she says she will accept £13,500. She also says she will keep her offer to them open until 12 o'clock on the following Monday, 13 December, if they each pay her £100. Chas and Dave agree and each hands over £100. On the Saturday before the deadline, Chas and Dave have to leave the country on business but before they do so, each post a letter stating that they agree to buy one of the prints at the agreed price of £13,500. Chas' letter arrives at 9.30 on the Monday morning but Dave's letter is delayed and arrives on the morning of Tuesday 14 December.

Required

(a)   Identify whether the notice Ann placed in her gallery window is an offer or an invitation to treat

                                                                              (2 marks)

(b)   State whether Ann has entered into a binding contract with Chas   **(2 marks)**

(c)   State whether Ann has entered into a binding contract with Dave   **(2 marks)**

                                                                              (Total = 6 marks)

8.2   Ace Ltd placed the following notice in the January edition of its company journal to request help in solving a problem with one of its computer products – the Brag: '£10,000 reward to any employee who can design a solution to the Brag problem before 1 April.'

Cid, who was married to an employee of Ace Ltd, read the journal and thought that he could solve the problem, so started work on it. Ed, employed by Ace Ltd, also saw the advert and decided to work on it. Ed solved the problem, but before he could notify Ace Ltd, the company decided to cancel the Brag product and placed a note in the March edition of its journal cancelling the reward.

Required

(a)   Identify whether an offer of reward creates a unilateral or bilateral contract   **(2 marks)**

(b)   State whether Cid has any right of action against Ace Ltd for the work that he did in attempting to solve the Brag problem   **(2 marks)**

(c)   State whether Ed has any right of action against Ace Ltd for the work that he did in solving the Brag problem   **(2 marks)**

                                                                              (Total = 6 marks)

8.3   Zri operates a business as a designer of internet web pages for a variety of business clients. Unfortunately he has had some difficulty in recovering his full fees from a number of clients as follows:

Ad, a self-employed car mechanic, without contacting Zri, simply sent him a cheque for half of his fees stating that he could not pay any more and that the cheque was in full settlement of his outstanding debt. Zri rang Ad about this and reluctantly agreed to waive half the fees.

Bi, a newly qualified accountant, told Zri that although she could only raise the cash to pay half of the outstanding fees she would, as an alternative to paying the other half, do all of Zri's accountancy work for the coming year. Zri reluctantly agreed to this proposal.

Cas, a self-employed musician, told Zri that she could not pay any of the money she owed him. However, her father offered to pay Zri, but could only manage half of the total amount owed. Once again Zri reluctantly agreed to accept the father's payment of the reduced sum.

Required

(a)   Explain whether Zri can claim his outstanding fees from Ad   **(2 marks)**

(b)   Explain

        (i)   Whether Zri can claim his outstanding fees from Bi

        (ii)   Whether Zri can claim his outstanding fees from Cas   **(4 marks)**

                                                                              (Total = 6 marks)

8.4 Whilst at work, Andy always parked his car in a car park operated by Bash Ltd. On the entry to the car park there is a large sign that states:

'Clients use these facilities strictly at their own risk and Bash Ltd accepts no liability whatsoever for any damage or injury sustained by either those using this facility or their vehicles or property, no matter how caused.'

Andy was aware of the sign, but had never paid much attention to it. However, one day he returned to his car to find that it had been badly damaged by a towing vehicle driven by an employee of Bash Ltd. Whilst on his way to the car park office to complain, he was hit by the same towing vehicle. As a result, not only was his car severely damaged, but he suffered a broken leg and was off work for eight weeks.

Bash Ltd has accepted that its employee was negligent on both counts but denies any liability, relying on the exclusion clause.

Required

(a)   State the nature of an exclusion clause   **(2 marks)**

(b)   Explain whether Andy can claim damages from Bash Ltd in respect of:
        (i)   The damage to his car
        (ii)   The injury to his leg   **(4 marks)**
                                                                                                    (Total = 6 marks)

8.5 Roger regularly takes part in a sport that involves fighting with wooden sticks. He has been successful in many fights but recently took part in one in which he lost to Jack. The fight took place under the necessary safety regulations and was stopped before Roger was hurt too badly. However, soon after the fight, it was clear that he had received severe brain damage and he now has difficulty talking.

Lulu used a public toilet at her local train station. Unfortunately the lock was defective and she was stuck inside. In a hurry to escape, she attempted to climb out of the window (despite a warning notice not to do so) and fell to the ground outside, injuring her head.

Required

(a)   Identify the elements that a claimant must prove to be owed a duty of care in a negligence claim
                                                                                                    (2 marks)

(b)   State whether the fight organiser has any defence to a negligence claim by Rodger   **(2 marks)**

(c)   State whether the train station has any defence to a negligence claim by Lulu   **(2 marks)**

                                                                                                    (Total = 6 marks)

                                                                                                    (Total = 30 marks)

9 Contract of employment

9.1 Which of the following describes the type of contract that an employee has?

A A contract of service
B A contract for services
C A contract of agency

(1 mark)

9.2 Which of the following factors indicates that a person is self-employed rather than an employee?

A The person owns their own tools
B The person is paid a salary net of tax
C The person may not delegate their obligations to someone else

(1 mark)

9.3 Which of the following is a consequence of being self-employed rather than employed?

A In the event of the employer's bankruptcy, the person has preferential rights as a creditor
B The person can register for and charge VAT
C The person is entitled to remedies for unfair dismissal

(1 mark)

9.4 Which of the following statements concerning employment contracts is correct?

A Employment contracts must be in writing
B Consideration is not required in an employment contract
C Employment contracts may include terms implied by custom and practice of the industry

(1 mark)

9.5 Which of the following is a common law duty of an employee?

A Obedience to all employer instructions
B To hold a reasonable level of qualifications
C To take reasonable care and skill in performing their work

(1 mark)

9.6 Which of the following is NOT a common law duty of an employer?

A To pay reasonable remuneration
B To provide health insurance
C To pay the employee if no work is available

(1 mark)

9.7 In which of the following situations is an employee entitled to time off work on full pay?

A A employee who wishes to leave the employer and look for another job
B A trade union member wishing to attend a trade union meeting
C A trade union official wishing to carry out trade union duties

(1 mark)

9.8 With regard to the tests applied by the courts to determine whether a person is an employee or self-employed, which of the following describes the focus of the integration test?

A Does the employer have control over how the person does their work?
B Is the employee so skilled that they cannot be controlled in the performance of their duties?
C Does the person work on their own account?
D How long has the person worked for the employer?

(2 marks)

9.9 Which of the following individual's below can be considered an employee?

A David – who invoices his employer and is paid gross
B Sally – who may delegate her work to others
C Rob – who is provided with his work tools by his employer
D Jane – who chooses the hours that she works

(2 marks)

9.10   Which TWO of the following are consequences of being an employee rather than self-employed?

(1)   The person does not have protection from unfair dismissal
(2)   The employer is vicariously liable for the tortious acts of the employee performed in the course of employment
(3)   PAYE tax is deducted by the employer from the employee's salary
(4)   The person is a non-preferential creditor in the event of the liquidation of the employer

A   1 and 2
B   1 and 4
C   2 and 3
D   3 and 4   **(2 marks)**

9.11   Which of the following statements concerning statutory employment protection is NOT correct?

A   The employed are entitled to protection from unfair dismissal
B   The self-employed are entitled to a minimum notice period
C   The employed are entitled to a minimum wage
D   The self-employed are entitled to protection of their health and safety   **(2 marks)**

9.12   Within how many months following the commencement of employment must the employer provide an employee with a written statement of prescribed particulars?

A   1 month
B   2 months
C   3 months
D   6 months   **(2 marks)**

9.13   Which of the following is NOT a right granted to employees in relation to new children?

A   Maternity pay
B   Paternity pay
C   Adoption leave
D   Workplace childcare   **(2 marks)**

9.14   Which of the following is NOT a right granted to a pregnant employee?

A   Time-off for ante-natel care
B   Protection from unfair dismissal
C   Statutory maternity leave
D   Flexible working on return to work   **(2 marks)**

9.15   Which TWO of the following are statutory rights that an employer owes their employees?

(1)   An itemised pay slip
(2)   A minimum hourly wage
(3)   Paid parental leave for parents of children up to the age of 5
(4)   A maximum working week of 45 hours

A   1 and 2
B   1 and 4
C   2 and 3
D   2 and 4   **(2 marks)**

(Total = 23 marks)

10 Dismissal and redundancy

10.1 What is the minimum period of notice that an employee with ten years of continuous service is entitled to?

    A   One week
    B   Two weeks
    C   Ten weeks   **(1 mark)**

10.2 Which of the following types of dismissal occurs when no notice is given to the employee?

    A   Constructive dismissal
    B   Summary dismissal
    C   Unfair dismissal   **(1 mark)**

10.3 An employee can seek damages for wrongful dismissal in which of the following circumstances?

    A   When they are dismissed unfairly but with the correct notice period
    B   When they are dismissed fairly with the correct notice period
    C   When they are summarily dismissed without justification   **(1 mark)**

10.4 Which of the following statements regarding wrongful dismissal is correct?

    A   A wrongfully dismissed employee is expected to mitigate their loss by seeking alternative employment
    B   Damages for wrongful dismissal include lost salary plus a sum for mental distress
    C   Cases for wrongful dismissal are heard by the criminal courts   **(1 mark)**

10.5 Which of the following is an exception to the rule that an employee must have a minimum period of continuous service to be protected from unfair dismissal?

    A   Pregnancy of the employee
    B   Disability of the employee
    C   Trade union membership of the employee   **(1 mark)**

10.6 Which of the following statements regarding compensation for unfair dismissal is correct?

    A   A compensatory award is not subject to a statutory maximum
    B   A basic award is determined by the age, salary and length of service of the employee and is subject to a statutory maximum
    C   An additional award may be granted for any reason at the tribunal's discretion   **(1 mark)**

10.7 In order to be entitled to redundancy pay, how long must an employee be continuously employed?

    A   1 year
    B   1.5 years
    C   2 years   **(1 mark)**

10.8 If an employee has ten years of continuous service with an employer, what is the minimum notice period that they need to give the employer if they decide to leave?

    A   One week
    B   Ten days
    C   One month
    D   Ten weeks   **(2 marks)**

10.9   Which of the following statements describes constructive dismissal?

    A   The employer dismissing the employee without the correct notice period and justification

    B   The employer dismissing the employee without any notice

    C   The employee resigns after they are required to work 40 hours per week when they are contracted to work 30

    D   The employee resigns after they are not awarded a discretionary bonus   **(2 marks)**

10.10 Which TWO of the following are justifiable reasons for summary dismissal?

    (1)   Misconduct

    (2)   Gross negligence

    (3)   Lateness

    (4)   Failure to follow a dress code

    A   1 and 2

    B   1 and 3

    C   2 and 3

    D   2 and 4   **(2 marks)**

10.11 Which of the following remedies are available to the employee in the event that they are wrongfully dismissed?

    A   Damages

    B   Re-engagement

    C   Re-instatement

    D   Statutory compensation   **(2 marks)**

10.12 In order to proceed with a claim for unfair dismissal, the employee must show that they were dismissed.

Which of the following is NOT counted as dismissal for unfair dismissal purposes?

    A   Employee resigning

    B   Constructive dismissal

    C   Expiry of a fixed-term contract without renewal

    D   Summary dismissal   **(2 marks)**

10.13 For unfair dismissal purposes, which of the following is a fair reason for dismissal?

    A   Pregnancy

    B   Trade union membership

    C   Lack of capability or qualifications

    D   Taking steps to avert a danger to health and safety at work   **(2 marks)**

10.14 Which of the following statements regarding compensation for unfair dismissal is NOT correct?

    A   Compensation may be reduced if it is just and equitable to do so

    B   Compensation may be reduced if it is greater than lost earnings

    C   Compensation may be reduced if the employee contributed to their own dismissal

    D   Compensation may be reduced if the employee unreasonably refused an offer of reinstatement

    (2 marks)

10.15 Which TWO of the following are circumstances where an employee will NOT be entitled to claim a redundancy payment?

(1)   They could have been dismissed for misconduct before the redundancy notice
(2)   Their claim is not made within 3 months of the redundancy notice
(3)   They are involved in strike action after the redundancy notice is served
(4)   They unreasonably refuse a renewal to their contract

A   1 and 3
B   1 and 4
C   2 and 3
D   2 and 4

(2 marks)

(Total = 23 marks)

11 MTQ Bank 2

36 mins

11.1 Gem Ltd has a number of different types of worker that perform services for it.

The 'professionals' are highly-skilled individuals who perform services for clients of Gem Ltd at a range of different locations owned by the company. Clients have the right to choose which professional they see and at what time.

The 'techies' are skilled technical workers that develop and maintain Gem Ltd's information systems. They are not told what work needs to be done, but are expected to identify and solve problems that arise. The order in which jobs are done and how the jobs are done is a decision for each 'techie'.

The 'greasemonkees' are unskilled workers who maintain the fleet of Gem Ltd's company vehicles. They are provided with the tools they need to do their job and are provided with a list of work that needs doing each day.

Required

(a)   State whether the 'professionals' are employees or independent contractors   **(2 marks)**
(b)   State whether the 'techies' are employees or independent contractors   **(2 marks)**
(c)   State whether the 'greasemonkees' are employees or independent contractors   **(2 marks)**

(Total = 6 marks)

11.2 Fine Ltd specialises in providing software to the financial services industry. It has two offices, one in Edinburgh and the other, its main office, in London. In January 20X3, Gus was employed as a software designer attached to the Edinburgh office. However, in May 20X4, Gus was informed that he was to be transferred to the head office in London, which is more than 350 miles from his usual workplace.

Gus refused to accept the transfer on the basis that he had been employed to work in Edinburgh not London. Consequently, on 1 June 20X4 he wrote to Fine Ltd terminating his contract with them.

Required

(a)   Explain constructive dismissal with regard to the termination of an employment contract

(2 marks)
(b)   State TWO examples of constructive dismissal   **(2 marks)**
(c)   State whether Gus can claim compensation for unfair dismissal   **(2 marks)**

(Total = 6 marks)

11.3 Fawn Ltd manufactures clothes and sells them through its own retail shop. Grace, who is 33 years old, has been employed by Fawn Ltd for three years as manager of the shop. Grace has just been told that her services are no longer required, as Fawn Ltd has decided to close its store and concentrate solely on manufacturing.

Required

(a)   Explain the nature of Grace's dismissal   **(2 marks)**
(b)   State the rules concerning other employment as an alternative to a redundancy payment

(2 marks)
(c)   State how Grace's statutory redundancy payment will be calculated (the actual calculation is not required)   **(2 marks)**

(Total = 6 marks)

11.4 Dan operated a business for many years. Until recently, Eve and Fred both worked for Dan and were described as self-employed and paid tax as self-employed persons. Dan provided all of the computer equipment and software they needed to perform their jobs. Eve was required to work solely on the projects Dan provided, and she had to attend Dan's premises every day from 9am until 5pm.

Fred usually worked at home and was allowed to work on other projects. Fred could even arrange for his work for Dan to be done by someone else if he was too busy to do it personally.

After three years of employment, and as a result of a downturn in his business sector, Dan has told Eve and Fred that there will be no more work for them and that they will not receive any further payment or compensation from him for their loss of work.

Required

(a)	State how courts decide whether a person is employed or self employed	**(2 marks)**
(b)	Explain whether Fred can claim any compensation for the loss of his job	**(2 marks)**
(c)	Explain whether Eve can claim compensation for the loss of her job	**(2 marks)**
		(Total = 6 marks)

11.5 Impact College Ltd provides private tuition. The college is managed by Jack, who also has responsibility for personnel matters. Fred and Gale are amongst the 60 lecturers currently employed by Impact College Ltd. They have both worked for Impact College for the past six years.

Fred has been the staff trade union representative for the past three years and has had several confrontations with Jack as to the working conditions of the college's employees. Gale has been off work twice in the past four years on maternity leave, to Jack's stated annoyance, and is pregnant once again.

It has transpired that Fred and Gale are amongst the ten members of staff selected for dismissal by the college and they suspect that Jack has pursued a personal vendetta against them.

Required

(a)	Identify what an employer must prove to avoid being found liable for unfair dismissal	**(2 marks)**
(b)	Explain whether Fred can claim unfair dismissal	**(2 marks)**
(c)	Explain whether Gale can claim unfair dismissal	**(2 marks)**
		(Total = 6 marks)

(Total = 30 marks)

12 Agency law

12.1 The purpose of an agency relationship is to form a business contract between which of the following parties?

 A Agent and principal
 B Agent and third party
 C Principal and third party (1 mark)

12.2 In order to form an agency relationship by express agreement, what form should the agreement take?

 A Oral agreement only
 B Written agreement only
 C Either oral or written agreement (1 mark)

12.3 'Holding out' is a key element of which form of agency?

 A Agency by implied agreement
 B Agency by estoppel
 C Agency by necessity (1 mark)

12.4 Which type of agent authority is derived from what is usual or customary in the circumstances?

 A Express authority
 B Ostensible authority
 C Implied authority (1 mark)

12.5 When combined, which types of agent authority are known as an agent's actual authority?

 A Express and implied authority
 B Implied and ostensible authority
 C Express and apparent authority (1 mark)

12.6 Unless circumstances indicate otherwise, which party is NOT liable under a contract properly formed under an agency agreement?

 A Agent
 B Principal
 C Third party (1 mark)

12.7 Which of the following statements regarding agency law is correct?

 A An agent may not enforce a contract that they helped to form
 B A principal may sue their agent if the third party is in breach of contract
 C A third party and principal do not need be in direct contact for a binding contract between them to be formed (1 mark)

12.8 Which type of agent runs an accountancy practice?

 A Company director
 B Partner
 C Commercial agent
 D Promoter (2 marks)

12.9 Which of the following statements concerning a principal ratifying a contract formed by an agent is correct?

 A The principal need not have existed when the contract was made
 B The principal need not have had legal capacity when the contract was made
 C The principal must communicate their ratification of the contract clearly to the third party
 D At least half of the provisions of the contract must be ratified (2 marks)

12.10 Which TWO types of agency are formed without the agent's consent?

(1) Agency by implied agreement
(2) Agency by express agreement
(3) Agency by estoppel
(4) Agency by ratification

A   1 and 2
B   1 and 3
C   2 and 3
D   3 and 4   (2 marks)

12.11 In an emergency situation, a person may need to take control of another party's goods and deal with them appropriately.

What type of agency is this known as?

A   Agency by implied agreement
B   Agency by estoppel
C   Agency by ratification
D   Agency by necessity   (2 marks)

12.12 Which of the following is included in an agent's ostensible authority?

A   The authority that the third party expects the agent to have
B   The authority that the agent states that they have
C   The authority that is usual in the circumstances and what the principal impliedly gives the agent
D   The authority that the principal expressly gives the agent   (2 marks)

12.13 In which of the following circumstances will an agent's apparent authority arise?

A   When the principal tells the agent orally what the limit of their authority is
B   What a third party determines the agent's authority is from what is usual in the circumstances
C   When, without the principal being aware, an agent tells a third party what their authority is
D   Where a principal has represented a person to third parties as being their agent, despite not actually appointing the person as such   (2 marks)

12.14 In which of the following circumstances will an agency relationship NOT be terminated?

A   Bankruptcy of principal
B   Death of principal
C   Insanity of principal
D   Performance by the principal of their contractual obligations   (2 marks)

12.15 In which TWO of the following situations will an agent be liable on a contract?

(1) Where it is usual business practice for the agent to be liable
(2) Where the agent acts on their own behalf even though they purport to be acting for the principal
(3) Where the principal intends for the agent to take personal liability
(4) Where the third party agrees with the principal that the agent will be liable

A   1 and 2
B   1 and 3
C   2 and 3
D   3 and 4   (2 marks)

(Total = 23 marks)

13 Partnerships

13.1 Which of the following statements regarding partnerships is correct?

    A   A partnership must exist for more than a single business transaction

    B   The business must be profitable

    C   A partner can be an individual living person or a registered company   **(1 mark)**

13.2 In which form of partnership is there a partner that invests in the partnership but does not take part in the day-to-day running of the business?

    A   Unlimited liability partnership

    B   Limited partnership

    C   Limited Liability Partnership   **(1 mark)**

13.3 As a minimum, which of the following formalities is necessary to form an unlimited liability partnership?

    A   A written partnership agreement

    B   A decision by the partners to set up business together

    C   Registration of the partnership at Companies House   **(1 mark)**

13.4 A partner's actual authority to bind the partnership in a contract is determined by which of the following?

    A   The perception third parties have of the purpose of the partnership

    B   What is agreed between the partners

    C   The actual purpose of the partnership   **(1 mark)**

13.5 Which of the following describes the liability of new partners for partnership debts?

    A   New partners are ordinarily liable for all partnership debts

    B   New partners are ordinarily liable for partnership debts in existence when they became a partner

    C   New partners are ordinarily liable for partnership debts that occur after they become a partner   **(1 mark)**

13.6 Under the Partnership Act 1890, which of the following events will cause a partnership to be terminated?

    A   Loss of 50% of the partnership's capital

    B   The partnership incurring losses for three consecutive years

    C   Bankruptcy of a partner   **(1 mark)**

13.7 When a partnership is terminated, which of the following is paid off first from the funds raised from the sale of assets?

    A   External debts

    B   Loans from partners

    C   Partners' capital contributions   **(1 mark)**

13.8 Which of the following statements regarding Limited Liability Partnerships is correct?

    A   A written partnership agreement is required to form the partnership

    B   The partnership dissolves when a partner leaves

    C   The partnership must have two designated members who are responsible for the publicity requirements of the partnership

    D   The partnership is exempt from audit   **(2 marks)**

13.9 Which of the following is true regarding Limited Liability Partnerships?

    A   The partnership is liable for its own debts
    B   The partnership does not need to file accounts with the Registrar of Companies
    C   One partner may not take part in the day-to-day running of the partnership
    D   Where the partnership cannot pay its own debts, the partners are jointly liable up to an amount they have guaranteed

(2 marks)

13.10 When forming an unlimited liability partnership, a partnership agreement may be written.

Which TWO statements regarding written partnership agreements are correct?

    (1)   Terms in the agreement override terms implied by the Partnership Act 1890
    (2)   Written partnership agreements are required by law where there are more than 20 partners in the partnership
    (3)   Written partnership agreements must be in the form of a deed
    (4)   Written partnership agreements are not required on formation and may be created at any point in the life of the partnership

    A   1 and 2
    B   1 and 4
    C   2 and 3
    D   3 and 4

(2 marks)

13.11 Which of the following is true concerning partnerships and legal charges?

    A   Partnerships can grant fixed charges only
    B   Partnerships can grant floating charges only
    C   Partnerships can grant both fixed and floating charges
    D   Partnerships cannot grant fixed or floating charges

(2 marks)

13.12 Which of the following statements concerning retiring partners is correct?

    A   Retiring partners are not liable for any partnership debts after they leave
    B   Retiring partners are liable only for existing partnership debts when they leave, unless third parties are notified that they have retired
    C   Retiring partners are responsible for existing partnerships debts when they leave and partnership debts incurred after their retirement, unless third parties are notified of their retirement
    D   Retiring partners are only liable for partnership debts incurred after they leave

(2 marks)

13.13 Which of the following is necessary to terminate a Limited Liability Partnership?

    A   It must be formally wound-up
    B   A court order
    C   An order from the Registrar of Companies
    D   A deed signed by the partners

(2 marks)

13.14 When an unlimited liability partnership is terminated, which of the following is paid off last out of funds realised from the partnership assets?

    A   Partners' share of partnership profits
    B   Partners' capital contribution
    C   Partnership loans
    D   External debts

(2 marks)

13.15 Under the Partnership Act 1890, which TWO of the following events will terminate an unlimited liability partnership?

(1) Notice by a partner
(2) The end of an agreed fixed period of time for the partnership
(3) Absence of a partner
(4) Disagreement between the partners

A   1 and 2
B   1 and 3
C   2 and 3
D   3 and 4

(2 marks)

(Total = 23 marks)

14 Corporations and legal personality

14.1 Which of the following is a benefit of running a business as a sole trader?

   A   No formal procedures to set up the business
   B   The business is highly dependant on the owner
   C   An absence of economies of scale   **(1 mark)**

14.2 Which of the following statements regarding sole traders is correct?

   A   The business is legally distinct from the owner
   B   All of a sole trader's profits accrue to the owner
   C   Sole traders do not need to register for VAT   **(1 mark)**

14.3 In a company limited by shares, what is the limit of a member's liability?

   A   The amount they guaranteed to pay in the event of the company being wound-up
   B   The amount of share capital they have purchased, including any amounts outstanding on the shares
        that they own
   C   Nothing, the company is liable for its own debts   **(1 mark)**

14.4 Which type of company does not have share capital?

   A   An unlimited liability company
   B   A public company
   C   A company limited by guarantee   **(1 mark)**

14.5 How much is the minimum issued share capital of a public company?

   A   £12,500
   B   £25,000
   C   £50,000   **(1 mark)**

14.6 Which of the following is an effect of a company's separate legal personality?

   A   Members and directors of a company are protected from the force of the law
   B   The company is liable for its own debts
   C   Members have no liability in the event of the company being insolvent   **(1 mark)**

14.7 In which of the following situations will the courts lift the veil of incorporation?

   A   Where a director commits fraudulent trading
   B   Where a member of a solvent company fails to pay the company what is outstanding on their share
        capital
   C   Where an employee commits a tort in the course of their employment   **(1 mark)**

14.8 Which of the following indicates that a business is being run as a sole trader?

   A   The business does not employ any employees
   B   It does not file accounts with the Registrar of Companies
   C   The business is run by one person who is not legally distinct from the business
   D   Share capital of the business are not sold on a recognised stock exchange **(2 marks)**

14.9 A group of friends wish to set up a business. They wish to limit their liability for the business' debts to an
     amount that they agree to when the business is formed.

     Which of the following businesses is most suitable to the needs of the group?

   A   An unlimited company
   B   A company limited by shares
   C   A partnership
   D   A corporation sole   **(2 marks)**

14.10 Which TWO of the following are true regarding public companies?

(1) A public company must have a minimum of two members
(2) A public company must have a minimum of two directors
(3) A public company cannot be an unlimited liability company
(4) A public company must have 'ltd' at the end of its name

A   1 and 2
B   2 and 3
C   2 and 4
D   3 and 4   **(2 marks)**

14.11 Which of the following is NOT a criteria that a company must meet if it is to qualify for the small companies' regime?

A   Balance sheet total of not more than £3.26 million
B   Net profit of no more than £1.0 million
C   Turnover of not more than £6.5 million
D   An average of 50 or fewer employees   **(2 marks)**

14.12 Which term is used to describe the type of company that has its shares traded on a public stock exchange?

A   Listed company
B   Public company
C   Private company
D   Unlimited company   **(2 marks)**

14.13 Which of the following statements regarding parent companies is NOT correct?

A   A company is a parent company if it holds the majority of the voting rights in another company
B   A company is a parent company if it has the right to exercise dominant influence over another company
C   A company is a parent company if it holds debentures in another company
D   A company is a parent company of any subsidiaries that its subsidiary company controls   **(2 marks)**

14.14 Which of the following statements in regards to a company's legal personality is correct?

A   Separate legal personality exempts members from liability if the company is liquidated
B   Separate legal personality only applies to private limited companies
C   Separate legal personality does not apply to unlimited liability companies
D   Separate legal personality can be ignored in certain circumstances   **(2 marks)**

14.15 In which TWO of the following circumstances may the veil of incorporation be lifted?

(1) To allow directors of insolvent companies to be found liable for the debts of the company
(2) To treat a group company as a single economic entity
(3) To allow an auditor access to company records
(4) To allow a private company to re-register as a public company

A   1 and 2
B   1 and 3
C   2 and 3
D   3 and 4   **(2 marks)**

(Total = 23 marks)

15 Company formation

15.1 Which of the following describes the general duty of a promoter?

A   Reasonable skill and care
B   Competence and accuracy
C   Due diligence   **(1 mark)**

15.2 Which of the following statements concerning pre-incorporation contracts is correct?

A   Pre-incorporation contracts must be ratified by the company
B   Pre-incorporation contracts cannot be ratified by the company
C   Pre-incorporation contracts can be ratified by the company if the third party agrees   **(1 mark)**

15.3 Which of the following parties is NOT liable on a pre-incorporation contract?

A   The company
B   The promoter
C   The third party   **(1 mark)**

15.4 Which of the following criteria must a public company meet before it can trade?

A   It must obtain a trading certificate from the Registrar of Companies
B   Its shares must be listed on a stock exchange
C   It must have appointed an auditor   **(1 mark)**

15.5 Which of the following criteria must a private company meet before it can trade?

A   It must have obtained a trading certificate from the Registrar of Companies
B   It must have obtained a certificate of incorporation from the Registrar of Companies
C   The members must have agreed to set up the company   **(1 mark)**

15.6 Which of the following company books is a public company NOT legally required to keep?

A   Register of charges
B   Register of debentureholders
C   Register of disclosed interests in shares   **(1 mark)**

15.7 Which of the following is true regarding a register of directors?

A   The register must include shadow directors
B   The register must be made available for inspection by company members for a fee
C   The register must include a service address for each director   **(1 mark)**

15.8 The role of which of the following parties is to form a company?

A   Subscriber
B   Member
C   Director
D   Promoter   **(2 marks)**

15.9 Which of the following statements concerning promoters is correct?

A   An accountant who acts in a professional capacity in the formation of a company is a promoter
B   A promoter may not make a profit as a result of their position
C   A promoter that acts as an agent for others must not put themselves into a position where their own interests clash with that of the company they are forming
D   A promoter may not own shares in the company that they are forming   **(2 marks)**

15.10 Which TWO of the following are methods that a promoter can use to avoid liability on pre-incorporation contracts?

(1)   Signing the pre-incorporation contract 'on behalf of the company'
(2)   Executing the pre-incorporation contract as a deed
(3)   Buying an 'off-the-shelf' company
(4)   Novating the contract

A   1 and 2
B   1 and 3
C   2 and 3
D   3 and 4   **(2 marks)**

15.11 To register a company, a number of documents must be submitted to the Registrar of Companies.

Which of the following is NOT a document that needs to be sent to the Registrar to register a company?

A   Articles of association
B   Memorandum of association
C   Statement of compliance
D   Statement of proposed officers   **(2 marks)**

15.12 A promoter sent the documents needed to register a company to the Registrar of Companies on 1/1/X1. The Registrar received the documents on 4/1/X1. The certificate of incorporation is dated 6/1/X1 and it is received by the promoter on 8/1/X1.

On which date was the company incorporated?

A   1/1/X1
B   4/1/X1
C   6/1/X1
D   8/1/X1   **(2 marks)**

15.13 In which of the following circumstances must a public company re-register as a private company?

A   If the market value of its shares falls below the nominal value of the shares
B   If it has makes trading losses for three consecutive years
C   If it fails to pay its corporation tax liability
D   If its share capital falls below £50,000   **(2 marks)**

15.14 Which of the following roles is NOT performed by the Registrar of Companies?

A   Issuing each company's Certificate of Incorporation
B   Registering companies that will be sold 'off-the-shelf'
C   Filing a copy of each company's Register of Members
D   Filing copies of each company's special resolutions   **(2 marks)**

15.15 Which TWO of the following correctly describe the requirements for private and public companies to keep accounting records?

(1)   Private companies must keep their accounting records for three years
(2)   Private companies must keep their accounting records for six years
(3)   Public companies must keep their accounting records for six years
(4)   Public companies must keep their accounting records for seven years

A   1 and 3
B   1 and 4
C   2 and 3
D   2 and 4   **(2 marks)**

(Total = 23 marks)

16 Constitution of a company

16.1 Which of the following parties signs a company's memorandum of association?

  A   The promoter
  B   The directors
  C   The subscribers   (1 mark)

16.2 Which of the following is true of model articles of association?

  A   Model articles of association describe how the company is to be managed and administered
  B   A company must only use the model articles of association that is relevant to its type of company
  C   The content of model articles of association cannot be amended by the members   (1 mark)

16.3 Which of the following is NOT something that would be found within model articles of association?

  A   Clauses relating to the rights of members
  B   Clauses relating to the transfer of shares
  C   Clauses relating to the mission statement of the company   (1 mark)

16.4 Which of the following statements regarding changing a company's articles of association is correct?

  A   A company may only change its articles once in a financial year
  B   A company requires a special or written resolution with a 75% majority to change its articles
  C   A company must send copies of the amended articles to the Registrar of Companies within 28 days
      of the amendment taking place   (1 mark)

16.5 Which of the following changes to a company's articles of association is void?

  A   Changes that allow a member additional votes so that they may block company resolutions on certain
      issues
  B   Changes that restrict the objects of the company
  C   Changes that conflict with the Companies Act   (1 mark)

16.6 Which of the following is a correct rule concerning company names?

  A   A company may be required to change its name if it is deemed offensive by the Secretary of State
  B   A company may not set its own rules for changing its name
  C   A company may not have a name that suggests a connection with the Government   (1 mark)

16.7 Are companies permitted to change their names and domiciles?

  A   A company may change its name but not its domicile
  B   A company may change its domicile but not its name
  C   A company may change its name and its domicile   (1 mark)

16.8 Which of the following parties is contractually bound by a company's constitution?

  A   The company
  B   Members in a capacity other than as a member
  C   Company directors
  D   Third parties with a business relationship with the company   (2 marks)

16.9 A company may have restricted objects and therefore it may not be permitted to enter into certain contracts.

Which of the following statements describes the position of third parties whose contract with a company is outside the scope of its objects?

A   The contract will not be a valid one
B   The company is required to ratify the contract for it to be binding on it
C   The contract will be binding on the company and the third party
D   The contract is voidable at the instance of the company   **(2 marks)**

16.10 Which TWO of the following are included in the content of a company's model articles of association?

(1)   Payment of dividends
(2)   Payment of charitable donations
(3)   Formation of a remuneration committee
(4)   Appointment of directors

A   1 and 2
B   1 and 4
C   2 and 3
D   2 and 4   **(2 marks)**

16.11 Which of the following is true regarding the content of model articles of association?

A   The content of model articles of association is the same for all types of company
B   The content of model articles of association includes clauses relating to the remuneration of employees
C   The content of model articles of association includes clauses relating to the ethical treatment of suppliers
D   The content of model articles of association includes clauses relating to communication with members   **(2 marks)**

16.12 Which of the following changes to a company's articles of association is valid?

A   Compelling a member to subscribe for additional shares
B   Permitting the company to perform an illegal act
C   Reducing the majority needed in a resolution to change the company's name to 25%
D   Complelling a member to accept increased liability on the company's shares that they hold   **(2 marks)**

16.13 Which of the following statements regarding members wishing to amend a company's articles of association is correct?

A   The change must be bona fide for the benefit of the company as a whole
B   A minority cannot prevent the majority from unjustly discriminating against them by changing the articles
C   The majority may not alter the articles if a minority feels it is prejudicial to their interests
D   A majority of members may not force a transfer of shares from the minority to themselveseven if it is in the best interests of the company as a whole   **(2 marks)**

16.14 Which of the following is true regarding the choice of company name?

A   No name may be offensive or sensitive as defined by the Secretary of State
B   All private companies must end their name with 'Ltd'
C   Names that suggest a connection with government are void
D   Companies that are registered as Welsh must end their name with '(Cym)'   **(2 marks)**

16.15 Which TWO statements concerning company names and passing-off action are correct?

(1) Only the Company Names Adjudicators can create a new company name, if one is needed, following a complaint about a company name that is too similar to another

(2) A passing-off action will fail if the claimant has not sought a remedy from the Company Names Adjudicators first

(3) A company can be prevented by a court injunction from using its name, even if it is properly registered

(4) Courts can refuse an injunction to prevent the use of a company name if the businesses are sufficiently different in nature

A   1 and 2
B   1 and 4
C   2 and 3
D   3 and 4

(2 marks)

(Total = 23 marks)

17 MTQ Bank 3

36 mins

17.1 Ham, Sam and Tam formed a partnership to run a petrol station. The partnership agreement expressly stated that the partnership business was to be limited exclusively to the sale of petrol.

In January 20X8 Sam received £10,000 from the partnership's bank drawn on its overdraft facility. He told the bank that the money was to finance a short-term partnership debt but in fact he used the money to pay for a round-the-world cruise. In February 20X8 Tam entered into a £15,000 contract on behalf of the partnership to buy a stock of bicycles, which he hoped to sell from the garage forecourt. In March 20X8 the partnership's bank refused to honour its cheque for the payment of its monthly petrol account, on the basis that there were no funds in its account and it had reached its overdraft facility.

Required

(a) Explain the liability of the partners for the bank overdraft **(2 marks)**
(b) Explain the liability of the partners for the contract to buy the bicycles **(2 marks)**
(c) Explain the liability of the partners for the petrol account **(2 marks)**

(Total = 6 marks)

17.2 Mick has operated a house building business as a sole trader for a number of years. The business is growing and in recent times, Mick has taken out a loan to buy business assets. Mick is considering tendering for a couple of very large contracts that should earn the business substantial sums, but also increases his potential liability if he is in breach of contract.

Now his accountant has recommended that he should consider registering as a company in order to gain the benefits of separate corporate personality.

Required

(a) State what is meant by separate corporate personality **(2 marks)**
(b) Explain why registering his business as a company may be of benefit to Mick **(4 marks)**

(Total = 6 marks)

17.3 Doc, a supplier of building materials, entered into the following transactions:

An agreement to sell some goods to a longstanding friend, Ed. The contractual document, however, actually stated that the contract was made with Ed's company, Ed Ltd. Although the materials were delivered, they have not been paid for and Doc has learned that Ed Ltd has just gone into insolvent liquidation.

Doc had employed a salesman, Fitt, whose contract of employment contained a clause preventing him from approaching any of Doc's clients for a period of two years after he had left Doc's employment. Doc has found out that, on stopping working for him, Fitt has started working for a company, Gen Ltd, wholly owned by Fitt and his wife, and is approaching contacts he had made while working for Doc.

Required

(a) Identify what is meant by limited liability **(2 marks)**
(b) Explain whether Doc can pursue Ed personally for the debts of Ed Ltd **(2 marks)**
(c) Explain whether the courts will lift the veil of incorporation to allow Doc to sue Fitt for breach of his employment contract **(2 marks)**

(Total = 6 marks)

17.4 Don was instrumental in forming Eden plc, which was registered and received its trading certificate in December 20X4. It has subsequently come to the attention of the board of directors that the following events had taken place prior to the incorporation of the company:

Don entered into a contract in the company's name to buy computer equipment, which the board of directors do not wish to honour.

Don entered into a contract in the company's name to develop a particular patent, which the board of directors of Eden wish to pursue but in relation to which the other party does not wish to proceed.

Don entered into an agreement with Fad Ltd for business equipment. The agreement was made 'subject to adoption by Eden plc' but now Eden plc does not wish to pursue the agreement.

Required

(a) Explain whether Eden plc is liable for the computer equipment contract **(2 marks)**
(b) Explain whether Eden can pursue the third party in relation to the patent contract **(2 marks)**
(c) Explain whether Don can claim reimbursement from Eden plc for the business equipment
(2 marks)
(Total = 6 marks)

17.5 Fred is a member of Glad Ltd, a small publishing company, holding 100 of its 500 shares; the other 400 shares are held by four other members. It has recently become apparent that Fred has set up a rival business to Glad Ltd and the other members have decided that he should be expelled from the company.

To that end, they propose to alter the articles of association to include a new power to 'require any member to transfer their shares for fair value to the other members upon the passing of a resolution so to do'.

Required

(a) State which parties are bound by a company's articles of association **(2 marks)**
(b) Explain the procedure that the members of Glad Ltd must follow in order to amend the company's articles **(2 marks)**
(c) Explain whether the other members of Glad Ltd will be successful in their attempt to change the articles and require Fred to transfer his shares to them **(2 marks)**
(Total = 6 marks)

(Total = 30 marks)

18 Share capital

18.1 As a minimum, how many members must a public company have?

    A   1
    B   2
    C   3   **(1 mark)**

18.2 Which of the following statements regarding ordinary share capital is correct?

    A   Dividends must be paid on ordinary share capital every financial year
    B   On liquidation of the company, ordinary shares entitle the shareholder to have their capital repaid ahead of other creditors
    C   Ordinary shares may or may not have voting rights attached   **(1 mark)**

18.3 Which of the following statements regarding treasury shares is correct?

    A   Only public limited companies may create treasury shares
    B   A company may exercise voting rights on its treasury shares
    C   Treasury shares may be reissued for cash without the usual issuing formalities   **(1 mark)**

18.4 Which of the following describes the public offer method of allotting shares by a public company?

    A   An offer to the public to apply for shares based on information in a prospectus
    B   Members of the public subscribe for shares directly to the company
    C   Shares are offered in a small number of large blocks to persons or institutions who have previously agreed to purchase the shares at a pre-determined price   **(1 mark)**

18.5 Which of the following describes a rights issue?

    A   An offer to existing shareholders to purchase further shares in the company
    B   The allotment of additional shares to existing shareholders in proportion to their holdings
    C   An offer to debentureholders to purchase shares in the company   **(1 mark)**

18.6 Which of the following statements regarding issuing shares is correct?

    A   Shares must be issued at their nominal value
    B   Shares may be issued at a discount to their nominal value
    C   Shares may be issued at a premium to their nominal value   **(1 mark)**

18.7 Which of the following is true concerning issuing shares?

    A   A company must receive full payment of the nominal value of a share when it is issued
    B   A shareholder who did not pay the full nominal value of their share on issue, must pay any unpaid amount before selling the share
    C   Where a shareholder did not pay the full nominal value of their share on issue, the debt transfers to the new shareholder if the share is sold   **(1 mark)**

18.8 Which of the following describes a company's called-up share capital?

    A   The amount the company has required shareholders to pay on existing shares
    B   The type, class, number and amount of shares issued and allotted to shareholders
    C   The amount shareholders have paid on existing shares
    D   The maximum amount of share capital that a company can have in issue   **(2 marks)**

18.9 Which of the following is correct concerning the market value of a company's shares?

    A   Market value must be greater than nominal value
    B   Market value must be lower than nominal value
    C   Market value equals nominal value
    D   Market value may be equal, greater or lower than nominal value   **(2 marks)**

18.10 Which TWO of the following statements regarding preference shares are correct?

(1) A company is compelled to pay dividends on preference shares every financial year
(2) Preference shares do not normally entitle the shareholder to vote in company meetings
(3) Preference shareholders usually have a right to have their capital returned in the event of a liquidation ahead of ordinary shareholders
(4) In the event of a liquidation, preference shareholders have the right to share in any surplus assets ahead of the ordinary shareholders

A   1 and 2
B   2 and 3
C   2 and 4
D   3 and 4   (2 marks)

18.11 With regard to share capital, which of the following constitutes a variation of class rights?

A   Issuing shares of the same class to allottees who are not already members of the class
B   Returning capital to preference shareholders
C   Subdividing shares of another class with the incidental effect of increasing the voting strength of that other class
D   Changing the amount of dividend payable to a class of preference share   (2 marks)

18.12 Which of the following is true regarding the power of directors to allot shares?

A   Directors of private companies with one class of share have the power to allot shares unless restricted by the articles
B   Directors of all private companies have the power to allot shares unless restricted by the articles
C   Directors of private and public companies with one class of share have the power to allot shares unless restricted by the articles
D   Directors of all private and public companies have the power to allot shares unless restricted by the articles   (2 marks)

18.13 Pre-emption rights are granted in which of the following situations?

A   A company proposes to allot ordinary shares wholly for cash
B   A company proposes to allot ordinary shares
C   A company proposes to allot preference shares wholly for cash
D   A company proposes to allot preference shares   (2 marks)

18.14 Which of the following statements regarding payment for shares is correct?

A   Public company shares must always be paid for in cash
B   At the time of allotment, a public company must receive payment of at least 50% of the nominal value of the shares
C   A private company may allot shares for inadequate consideration by accepting goods or services at an over-value
D   A private company must have non-cash consideration independently valued before accepting it as payment for shares   (2 marks)

18.15 Which TWO of the following are valid uses of a share premium account?

   (1)   To issue fully paid shares under a bonus issue
   (2)   To pay issue costs and expenses in respect of a new share issue
   (3)   To issue fully paid shares under a rights issue
   (4)   To purchase treasury shares

   A   1 and 2
   B   1 and 4
   C   2 and 3
   D   2 and 4

(2 marks)

(Total = 23 marks)

19 Loan capital

19.1 Which of the following is true regarding the borrowing powers of companies?

A   All companies registered under the Companies Act 2006 have an implied power to borrow
B   The members of public companies registered under the Companies Act 2006 must authorise the company to borrow
C   The Companies Act 2006 sets a maximum limit on the amount each type of company may borrow

(1 mark)

19.2 In relation to debentures issued as a series, which of the following describes the term pari passu?

A   All debenutures rank equally
B   Older debentures rank above newer debentures
C   Higher value debentures rank above lower value debentures

(1 mark)

19.3 Which of the following differences between share capital and debentures is correct?

A   Dividend payments on shares is tax-deductible, interest payments on debentures is not tax-deductible
B   Interest payments on debentures is mandatory, dividend payments on shares is discretionary
C   In the event of liquidation, shareholders are paid their investment back before the debentureholders

(1 mark)

19.4 Which of the following charges on the same asset, all of which have been properly registered, has the highest priority? Assume all chargeholders are unaware of the other charges.

A   A floating charge with a value of £5,000 registered on 1 January 20X1
B   A fixed charge with a value of £2,000 registered on 1 February 20X1
C   A floating charge with a value of £7,000 registered on 1 March 20X1

(1 mark)

19.5 Which of the following events will cause a floating charge to crystallise?

A   Resignation of the finance director
B   The chargee appointing a receiver
C   Sale of the assets subject to the charge

(1 mark)

19.6 How many days after creation must a charge be registered in order for it to be valid and enforceable?

A   7
B   14
C   21

(1 mark)

19.7 Which of the following is true concerning late registration of a company charge?

A   A charge may not be registered late
B   A charge may be registered late, but only if the permission of the Registrar of Companies is obtained
C   A charge may be registered late if it does not prejudice the creditors or shareholders of the company

(1 mark)

19.8 Which of the following statements regarding directors' borrowing powers is correct?

A   Where directors borrow for a non-business purpose, the loan contract is unenforceable by the lender
B   Where directors borrow a greater amount than they have the power to, the loan contract is unenforceable by the lender
C   Where directors exceed their powering powers, the company may ratify the loan contract if it is within the capacity of the company
D   Where directors borrow for a business purpose, the loan contract is unenforceable unless it is supported by a company charge

(2 marks)

19.9 Which of the following MUST be created using a debenture trust deed?

   A   A single debenture
   B   Debenture stock
   C   Series debentures
   D   Register of debentureholders   **(2 marks)**

19.10 Which TWO of the following are advantages of using a debenture trust deed?

   (1)   The deed creates a charge or charges over the company's assets which creates security
   (2)   A single trustee of the debentureholders is appointed so the company only has to deal with one person
   (3)   Debentures covered by a debenture trust deed have a higher priority of repayment on liquidation than debentures not covered by a deed
   (4)   The process of selling a debenture covered by a debenture trust deed is substantially faster than the process of selling a debenture not covered by a debenture trust deed.

   A   1 and 2
   B   1 and 4
   C   2 and 3
   D   3 and 4   **(2 marks)**

19.11 Which of the following statements regarding the differences between loan capital and share capital is correct?

   A   Unlike loan capital, share capital does not have to be repaid
   B   Loan capital has voting rights attached but share capital does not
   C   Share capital offers the holder more security than loan capital
   D   Share capital is transferrable but loan capital is not   **(2 marks)**

19.12 Which of the following statements regarding the differences between loan capital and share capital is NOT correct?

   A   A shareholder is an owner of the company, a debentureholder is not
   B   Shares may not be issued at a discount to their nominal value, debentures may be issued at a discount to their nominal value
   C   An public sale of shares is known as a prospectus, the public sale of debentures is known as a listing
   D   There are statutory restrictions on redeeming shares, there are no statutory restrictions on redeeming debentures   **(2 marks)**

19.13 Which of the following is the purpose of a 'negative pledge' clause on a company charge?

   A   To prevent the company from issuing a subsequent charge on the same asset
   B   To prevent the company from selling the asset without the chargee's permission
   C   To prevent the company from using the asset without the chargee's permission
   D   To ensure the company pays the proceeds from the sale of the asset to the chargeholder   **(2 marks)**

19.14 The holder of a floating charge may protect their priority by including in the terms of the charge a clause that prevents the borrower from creating a fixed charge on the same asset.

   What is the name given to such a clause?

   A   Injunction clause
   B   Positive pledge clause
   C   Negative pledge clause
   D   Equitable clause   **(2 marks)**

19.15 Which TWO of the following are true concerning the registration of company charges?

(1) Charges must be registered within 21 days of creation
(2) If a charge is not registered on time then the company and its officers who created the charge are liable to a fine
(3) The Registrar of Companies is permitted to rectify a mistake in the registration documents of a charge with the permission of the chargeholder
(4) Non-registered charges are valid and enforceable with the permission of the Registrar of Companies

A   1 and 2
B   1 and 4
C   2 and 3
D   3 and 4

(2 marks)

(Total = 23 marks)

20 Capital maintenance and dividend law

28 mins

20.1 What is the principle of capital maintenance?

    A   Companies should not make payments out of capital to the detriment of creditors

    B   Companies should seek to maintain or increase their capital at all times

    C   Companies should maintain the ratio of their debt and equity capital   **(1 mark)**

20.2 Which of the following statements regarding reduction of capital is correct?

    A   A limited company requires a court order to cancel unissued shares

    B   A limited company requires a special resolution of its members to cancel unissued shares

    C   A limited company is permitted without restriction to cancel its unissued shares   **(1 mark)**

20.3 Which of the following is required to permit a private company to reduce its share capital without application to a court?

    A   A special resolution only

    B   A special resolution and a solvency statement from the directors

    C   Authority in the articles and an ordinary resolution   **(1 mark)**

20.4 Which of the following is required to permit a public company to reduce its share capital?

    A   A special resolution and a solvency statement from the directors

    B   A special resolution and court approval

    C   Authority in the articles and a special resolution   **(1 mark)**

20.5 Which type of dividend is paid by the issue of additional shares?

    A   Scrip dividends

    B   Capital dividends

    C   Equity dividends   **(1 mark)**

20.6 At which point before its payment does a dividend become a debt of the company?

    A   When it is declared by the company in general meeting

    B   When it is recorded in the financial statements

    C   When the company's bank receives the instruction to make the payment   **(1 mark)**

20.7 Which of the following is an undistributable reserve for the payment of a dividend?

    A   Accumulated realised profits

    B   Retained earnings

    C   Capital redemption reserve   **(1 mark)**

20.8 The rules of capital maintenance exist to primarily protect which of the following parties?

    A   A company's members

    B   A company's creditors

    C   A company's customers

    D   The government   **(2 marks)**

20.9 Which of the following is NOT a valid method that a company may use to reduce its share capital according to the Companies Act 2006?

    A   Pay off part of paid-up share capital out of surplus profits

    B   Extinguish liability on partly paid shares

    C   Buy back fully paid up share capital from shareholders using cash not surplus profit

    D   Cancel paid-up share capital that is no longer represented by assets   **(2 marks)**

20.10 Which TWO of the following are true concerning the issuing of a solvency statement by private companies in connection with a reduction of the company's share capital?

(1) A solvency statement must be made 15 days in advance of the meeting where the special resolution concerning the reduction will be voted on

(2) Only the Chairman and Finance Director of the company must be named on the statement.

(3) The statement must declare that there are no grounds to suspect the company will be unable to pay its debts for the next six months

(4) It is an offence to make a solvency statement without reasonable grounds for the opinion expressed in it

A 1 and 2
B 1 and 4
C 2 and 3
D 3 and 4   **(2 marks)**

20.11 Which of the following statements concerning public companies reducing their share capital is correct?

A A public company can reduce its share capital to below £50,000 and remain a public company without restriction

B A public company that wishes to reduce its share capital to below £50,000 must re-register as a private company

C A public company that wishes to reduce its share capital to below £50,000 must obtain permission from the stock market

D A public company that wishes to reduce its share capital to below £50,000 must pass a written resolution of the members   **(2 marks)**

20.12 What is the name given to dividends that are paid part of the way through a company's financial year?

A Semi-dividends
B Dividends paid in specie
C Interim dividends
D Preference dividends   **(2 marks)**

20.13 In relation to the payment of dividends, which of the following will be included in the profit available for distribution in a company's current financial year?

A An increase in the asset value of a head office building that occurred during the current financial year
B Profit on the sale of an asset sold after the end of the current financial year
C A depreciation charge made in the current financial year
D A premium receieved on the nominal value of shares issued in the current financial year

(2 marks)

20.14 Which of the following statements is true concerning the payment of dividends by a public company?

A A public company may make a distribution as long as its net assets are not less than its share capital
B A public company may make a distribution as long as its net assets are not less than its undistributable reserves
C A public company may make a distribution as long as its net assets are not less than its share capital less its undistributable reserves
D A public company may make a distribution as long as its net assets are not less than its share capital plus its undistributable reserves   **(2 marks)**

20.15 Which TWO of the following statements concerning liability for the payment of unlawful dividends is correct?

(1) Directors are liable if they declare a dividend that they know to be paid out of capital
(2) Members who did not know the payment was unlawful are not liable
(3) Directors face criminal liability if they declare unlawful dividends
(4) Directors who honestly rely on proper accounts when deciding whether to pay a dividend are still liable if it turns out to be unlawful

A   1 and 2
B   1 and 4
C   2 and 3
D   3 and 4   (2 marks)

(Total = 23 marks)

21 MTQ Bank 4

21.1 Riz is considering incorporating a public limited company. He is keen to ensure that the company is funded correctly, but not excessively, and is aware that the Companies Act includes a number of rules concerning share capital.

He has been advised to consider the following terms in connection with share capital and is seeking your advice.

(1)   Issued share capital
(2)   Paid-up share capital
(3)   Called-up share capital
(4)   Authorised share capital

Required

(a)   Identify which concerns the number of shares held by shareholders   **(2 marks)**
(b)   Identify which concerns the amount of money a company has receieved for the shares held by shareholders   **(2 marks)**
(c)   State the rules concerning the minimum amount of issued and paid-up share capital of a public limited company   **(2 marks)**

(Total = 6 marks)

21.2 Flop Ltd was in financial difficulties. In January, in order to raise capital, it issued 10,000 £1 shares to Gus, but only asked him to pay 75p per share at the time of issue. The directors of Flop Ltd intended asking Gus for the other 25p per share at a later date. However, in June it realised that it needed even more than the £2,500 it could raise from Gus' existing shareholding. So in order to persuade Gus to provide the needed money Flop Ltd told him that if he bought a further 10,000 shares he would only have to pay a total of 50p for each £1 share, and it would write off the money owed on the original share purchase.

Gus agreed to this, but the injection of cash did not save Flop Ltd and in December it went into insolvent liquidation, owing a considerable amount of money.

Required

(a)   Explain the general rule concerning the issuing of shares at a discount to their nominal value
                                                                                                                          (2 marks)
(b)   Explain the extent of Gus's liability on the 10,000 £1 shares that he paid 75p each for   **(2 marks)**
(c)   Explain the extent of Gus's liability on the further 10,000 £1 shares that he paid 50p each for
                                                                                                                          (2 marks)

(Total = 6 marks)

21.3 In 20X5 two newspaper companies, Kudos Ltd and Lux Ltd, entered into an agreement in an attempt to safeguard their independent positions. Under the agreement, Kudos Ltd purchased 20% of Lux Ltd's preference shares which carry a preferred dividend of 10%.

The board of directors of Lux Ltd have recently become disenchanted with their link with Kudos Ltd and want encourage Kudos Ltd to sell its preference share in the company. To do this, the board of Lux Ltd proposes to reduce the dividend on all preference shares to 5%.

Required

(a)   State what is meant by the term class rights   **(2 marks)**
(b)   Explain the rules relating to the variation of class rights and whether Kudos Ltd can prevent the reduction of the preference dividend   **(4 marks)**

(Total = 6 marks)

21.4 Milly Ltd has recently entered into the following arrangements with its creditors.

(1) A single debenture of £15,000 from B Bank that is secured by a charge over Milly Ltds's trade receivables. Milly Ltd may deal with the trade receivables as it wishes. The charge documentation describes the charge as a fixed charge.

(2) A single debenture of £20,000 from Peppa Ltd secured on Milly Ltd's inventory. A floating charge was created on 3 March 20X1 and registered on 31 March 20X1.

(3) A single debenture of £5,000 from Otto Ltd that is also secured on Milly Ltd's inventory. A floating charge was created on 10 April 20X1 and registered on 30 April 20X1.

Required

(a) State whether Milly Ltd is required to keep a register of debenture holders in respect of the three debentures **(2 marks)**

(b) Identify the type of charge that was created over Milly Ltd's trade receivables **(2 marks)**

(c) State which of the floating charges will take priority if Milly Ltd is liquidated **(2 marks)**

(Total = 6 marks)

21.5 Dee and Eff are major shareholders in, and the directors of, Fan Ltd. For the year ended 30 April 20X8 Fan Ltds's financial statements showed a loss of £2,000 for the year and no profits were carried forward. For the year ended 30 April 20X9 Fan Ltd made a profit of £3,000. Also, due to a revaluation, the value of its land and buildings increased by £5,000. As a consequence, Dee and Eff recommended, and the shareholders approved, the payment of £4,000 in dividends.

Required

(a) Explain the legality of the dividend payment **(4 marks)**

(b) State the extent of Dee and Eff's liability regarding the dividend payment **(2 marks)**

(Total = 6 marks)

(Total = 30 marks)

22 Company directors

22.1 Which of the following types of director is expressly appointed as such?

A   De jure
B   De facto
C   Shadow

(1 mark)

22.2 What is the minimum age that a director can be?

A   16
B   17
C   18

(1 mark)

22.3 How many directors are required to retire at the first annual general meeting of a public company?

A   One-third of the directors
B   Half the directors
C   All of the directors

(1 mark)

22.4 Which of the following describes the actual authority of a Chief Executive Officer?

A   The authority that the board expressly gives to them
B   The authority that is usual for a Chief Executive Officer
C   The authority that the Chief Executive Officer says to others they have

(1 mark)

22.5 The powers of a company's directors are defined in which company document?

A   Articles of Association
B   Memorandum of Association
C   Register of Directors

(1 mark)

22.6 To which of the following does a director owe their statutory duties?

A   The members personally
B   The company as a whole
C   The board of directors

(1 mark)

22.7 In which of the following circumstances will a director be personally liable for the debts of the company?

A   Where the company's Articles of Association state that they are liable
B   Where a creditor has told them they are liable
C   Where they have breached their fiduciary duties

(1 mark)

22.8 Which of the following types of director is not validly appointed but is held out by the company to be a director?

A   De jure director
B   De facto director
C   Shadow director
D   Alternate director

(2 marks)

22.9 Which of the following is a characteristic of a non-executive director?

A   They are individuals that are held out by the company to be directors
B   They are not involved in the day-to-day running of the company
C   They are individuals whose instructions concerning running the company are followed
D   They are not subject to the statutory duties of directors

(2 marks)

22.10 Which TWO of the following are grounds where a court MUST disqualify a director?

(1) Conviction of an indictable offence in connection with the management of a company
(2) Insolvency of a company that they are a director of
(3) Conduct making them unfit to be concerned in the management of a company
(4) Persistently failing to meet provisions of company legislation

A 1 and 2
B 1 and 4
C 2 and 3
D 3 and 4 **(2 marks)**

22.11 Which of the following resolutions is required to remove a director from office?

A Ordinary resolution
B Ordinary resolution with special notice
C Special resolution
D Special resolution with special notice **(2 marks)**

22.12 Which of the following describes the correct way that directors should use their powers?

A For any reason necessary to maximise profit
B To achieve the goals of the business
C For a proper purpose that is honestly believed to be in the best interests of the company
D For any legal purpose **(2 marks)**

22.13 Which of the following statements concerning a director that has acted outside their authority is correct?

A The company many not subsequently ratify their actions
B The members may ratify their actions but an ordinary resolution is required
C The members may ratify their actions but a special resolution is required
D The board of directors can ratify their actions on behalf of the members **(2 marks)**

22.14 Which of the following statutory duties is a director meeting when they consider the long-term consequences of a decision on their employees?

A Act within powers
B Exercise independent judgement
C Avoid conflicts of interest
D Promote the success of the company **(2 marks)**

22.15 Which TWO of the following describe the level of knowledge, skill and experience required by a director in order to meet their statutory duty to exercise reasonable, skill, care and diligence?

(1) The knowledge, skill and experience that the director actually has
(2) The knowledge, skill and experience expected of the director by the board of directors
(3) The knowledge, skill and experience that is reasonably expected of a person carrying out the functions of the director
(4) The knowledge, skill and experience that the members of the company believe the director to actually have

A 1 and 3
B 1 and 4
C 2 and 3
D 2 and 4 **(2 marks)**

(Total = 23 marks)

23 Other company officers

23.1 Which of the following companies MUST have a company secretary?

    A   Private limited company
    B   Unlimited liability company
    C   Public limited company   **(1 mark)**

23.2 Which of the following parties associated with a company may NOT act as its company secretary?

    A   A company's sole director
    B   A company's accountant
    C   A company's solicitor   **(1 mark)**

23.3 Which of the following parties associated with a company appoints the company secretary?

    A   The members
    B   The directors
    C   The auditor   **(1 mark)**

23.4 Which of the following is eligible to act as a company's auditor?

    A   An employee of the company
    B   The partner of an employee of a company
    C   The accountancy firm responsible for producing the company's accounts   **(1 mark)**

23.5 Which of the following parties appoints the company's first ever auditors?

    A   The members
    B   The Registrar of Companies
    C   The directors   **(1 mark)**

23.6 Which of the following auditors are deemed automatically reappointed each year unless specific circumstances dictate otherwise?

    A   Auditors of public limited companies
    B   Auditors of private limited companies
    C   Auditors of quoted companies   **(1 mark)**

23.7 Which of the following is the statutory duty of an auditor?

    A   To report to the members that the accounts are accurate and free from error
    B   To report to the members that the accounts give a true and fair view and have been properly prepared in accordance with the Companies Act
    C   To report to the members that the accounts have been prepared in line with accounting standards   **(1 mark)**

23.8 Which of the following sets the specific duties expected of a company's secretary?

    A   The Articles of Association
    B   The Companies Act
    C   The Memorandum of Association
    D   The Board of Directors   **(2 marks)**

23.9 Which of the following contracts does a company secretary have the power to bind their company in?

    A   Purchase of inventory from a supplier
    B   Acquisition of a head office building
    C   Car hire for transporting customers to meetings with the directors
    D   A bank loan   **(2 marks)**

23.10 Which TWO of the following duties would a company secretary expect to perform?

(1) Establishing and maintaining the company's statutory registers
(2) Filing accurate returns with the Registrar of Companies.
(3) Hiring and firing directors
(4) Reviewing the work of the company auditor

A   1 and 2
B   1 and 4
C   2 and 3
D   3 and 4   **(2 marks)**

23.11 Which of the following is a permitted qualification for a company secretary of a public limited company?

A   A business degree
B   Employment as a plc's secretary for two out of five years preceding appointment
C   Full membership of the ACCA
D   A qualifying law degree   **(2 marks)**

23.12 Which of the following is a statutory right of a company auditor?

A   To attend board meetings
B   To vote in the company's general meetings
C   To access, at all times, the books, accounts and vouchers of the company
D   To appoint non-executive directors   **(2 marks)**

23.13 What type of company resolution is required to remove an auditor?

A   Ordinary resolution
B   Ordinary resolution with special notice
C   Special resolution
D   Special resolution with special notice   **(2 marks)**

23.14 Which of the following must an auditor of a non-quoted company provide if they are removed from office at a general meeting?

A   A breakdown of their fees covering the period they acted as auditor
B   A list of recommendations to the members on how company procedures may be improved
C   A statement to members and creditors of whether there are circumstances that the auditor believes should be brought to their attention
D   An opinion on the performance of the company directors   **(2 marks)**

23.15 Which TWO of the following are criteria that a private company must meet to be exempt from audit?

(1) Turnover less than £6.5 million
(2) Balance sheet total less than £3.26 million
(3) Average number of employees less than 30
(4) Total long-term debt less than £4.5 million

A   1 and 2
B   1 and 4
C   2 and 3
D   3 and 4   **(2 marks)**

(Total = 23 marks)

24 Company meetings and resolutions

24.1 An annual general meeting must be held by which of the following companies?

    A   Public limited company
    B   Private limited company
    C   Company limited by guarantee   **(1 mark)**

24.2 Unless a shorter period is agreed by the members, how many days' notice must be given in respect of an annual general meeting?

    A   14
    B   21
    C   28   **(1 mark)**

24.3 How many days' notice is required for a meeting at which a special resolution is to be voted on?

    A   14
    B   21
    C   28   **(1 mark)**

24.4 As a minimum, what percentage of the votes is required to pass an ordinary resolution?

    A   50%
    B   51%
    C   75%   **(1 mark)**

24.5 As a minimum, what percentage of the members can agree to a shorter notice period in respect of a general meeting?

    A   51%
    B   75%
    C   90%   **(1 mark)**

24.6 What is the minimum percentage of the voting rights required by members to requisition a resolution at an annual general meeting?

    A   5%
    B   10%
    C   15%   **(1 mark)**

24.7 On a vote on a show of hands, how many votes is each member granted?

    A   One
    B   One per share held
    C   As many votes as their shareholding entitles them to   **(1 mark)**

24.8 Which of the following is included in the ordinary business of an annual general meeting?

    A   Changing the company's name
    B   Reducing the company's share capital
    C   Approving the payment of dividends
    D   Appointing an administrator   **(2 marks)**

24.9 In a general meeting, which of the following items of business would require a special resolution?

    A   Appointing a director
    B   Removing an auditor
    C   Ratifying the ultra vires actions of a director
    D   Altering the Articles of Association   **(2 marks)**

24.10 Which TWO of the following are correct differences between ordinary and special resolutions?

(1) The text of a special resolution must be set out in full in the notice conveyning the meeting. The text of an ordinary resolution does not

(2) A special resolution requires 21 days' notice. An ordinary resolution requires 14 days notice

(3) An ordinary resolution can be passed on a show of hands, but a special resolution requires a poll is taken

(4) Copies of special resolutions must always be sent to the Registrar of Companies. Ordinary resolutions do not generally have to be sent to the Registrar

A   1 and 2
B   1 and 4
C   2 and 3
D   3 and 4   (2 marks)

24.11 Which type of resolution can ONLY be passed by a private company?

A   Written resolution
B   Ordinary resolution
C   Special resolution
D   Special resolution with special notice   (2 marks)

24.12 Which of the following may NOT be achieved by written resolution?

A   Removal of an auditor
B   Alteration of the company's articles
C   Variation of class rights
D   Change to the company's name   (2 marks)

24.13 How many days' notice is required for a meeting where a resolution requires special notice?

A   21
B   28
C   30
D   35   (2 marks)

24.14 Where members hold sufficient voting rights to requisition a resolution at a general meeting, how much notice in advance of the meeting must they give the company?

A   One week
B   Two weeks
C   Four weeks
D   Six weeks   (2 marks)

24.15 Which TWO of the following are rights of a proxy at a general meeting?

(1) To vote on a show of hands but not a poll
(2) To speak at the meeting
(3) To requisition a resolution at the meeting
(4) To demand a poll

A   1 and 2
B   1 and 3
C   2 and 4
D   3 and 4   (2 marks)

                                                                                              (Total = 23 marks)

25 MTQ Bank 5

36 mins

25.1 Caz is a director of Dull plc, but she also carries out her own business as a wholesale supplier of specialist metals under the name of Era Ltd. Last year Dull plc entered into a contract to buy a large consignment of metal from Era Ltd. Caz attended the board meeting that approved the contract and voted in favour of it, without revealing any link with Era Ltd.

Required

(a)	State what is meant by a director's fiduciary duties	**(2 marks)**
(b)	Explain any of a director's statutory duties that Caz may have breached	**(4 marks)**
		(Total = 6 marks)

25.2 Katch Ltd is a small private company. Although there are three members of its board of directors, the actual day-to-day running of the business is left to one of them, Len, who simply reports back to the board on the business he has transacted. Len refers to himself as the Chief Executive Officer of Katch Ltd, although he has never been officially appointed as such.

Six months ago Len entered into a contract on Katch Ltd's behalf with Mo to produce some advertising material for the company. However Katch Ltd did not wish to proceed with the advertising campaign and the board of directors have refused to pay Mo, claiming that Len did not have the necessary authority to enter into the contract with him.

Required

(a)	Explain a director's express authority	**(2 marks)**
(b)	Explain a Chief Executive Officer's implied authority	**(2 marks)**
(c)	Explain whether Mo is entitled to payment from Katch Ltd in respect of the contract entered into by Len	**(2 marks)**
		(Total = 6 marks)

25.3 Boo was recently disqualified from acting as a company director under the Company Directors Disqualification Act 1986. She decided to continue trading and arranged for her daughter, Mills, to form a new company. On registration, Mills was appointed as a director, however, she would receive instruction on what to do from Boo's personal financial advisor, Beni, who is accustomed to act on Boo's orders. Beni was not appointed as a director but is identified as the company's managing director on all its official paperwork.

Required

(a)	State which of the parties is a de jure director	**(2 marks)**
(b)	State which of the parties is a de facto director	**(2 marks)**
(c)	State which of the parties is a shadow director	**(2 marks)**
		(Total = 6 marks)

25.4 Vic, a full ACCA member, is the sole director of Envy Ltd, a wholsesaler of books. Last year he employed Div, his solicitor, to act as Envy Ltd's company secretary. Vic believed that Div had all the necessary knowledge and experience needed to do the job. Whilst Vic was away on business, Div entered Envy Ltd into a contract with Green Ltd to buy a consignment of tablet computers that would be resold as electronic books. Vic was not happy about this and intends to avoid the contract with Green Ltd, remove Div as company secretary and appoint himself to the role.

Required

(a)	State whether Envy Ltd is required to have a company secretary	**(2 marks)**
(b)	State whether Envy Ltd is bound by the contract to buy the tablet computers	**(2 marks)**
(c)	State whether Vic is legally permitted to perform the role of company secretary	**(2 marks)**
		(Total = 6 marks)

25.5 Grave plc's year-end was on 31 December 20X7. Notice of it's annual general meeting was sent to shareholders on 1March 20X8 and it was to be held on 25 March 20X8. However, the date of the meeting was not convienient for 75% of the company's shareholders who decided that the meeting should be held on 10 March 20X8. The meeting took place on 10 March 20X8.

Later that year, the company's auditors decided to resign. They requested that a general meeting should be held so that they can inform the shareholders of the circumstances surrounding their resignation. The directors of Grave plc are not keen for such a meeting to be held and are refusing to organise it.

Required

(a) State the ordinary business dealt with at an annual general meeting **(2 marks)**

(b) State whether Grave plc's annual general meeting was called correctly **(2 marks)**

(c) State whether the directors of Grave plc are required to hold the general meeting as requested by the auditors **(2 marks)**

(Total = 6 marks)

(Total = 30 marks)

26 Insolvency and administration

28 mins

26.1 Which of the following parties applies for a company to be wound-up in a creditors' voluntary winding-up?

  A   The creditors
  B   The members
  C   The directors   **(1 mark)**

26.2 Which of the following determines whether a voluntary winding-up is a members' or creditors' voluntary winding-up?

  A   The solvency of the company
  B   A decision of the members
  C   A decision of the creditors   **(1 mark)**

26.3 Which of the following parties may apply to the court for the compulsory winding-up of a company?

  A   The company's auditor if they deem it necessary in the public interest
  B   A creditor who is owed more than £750 and who sent the company a written demand for it over three weeks ago and has not had a reply
  C   The Registrar of Companies if they have not received copies of the company's last three financial statements.   **(1 mark)**

26.4 In which of the following situations will the court order the compulsory winding-up of a company on the just and equitable ground?

  A   Where 50% of the members disagree with the actions of the directors
  B   When the main object of the company cannot be achieved
  C   Where the company has failed to pay its creditors for three months   **(1 mark)**

26.5 Which of the following parties has their interest paid last out of a liquidated company's assets?

  A   Employees
  B   Unsecured creditors
  C   Members   **(1 mark)**

26.6 In the context of corporate insolvency, which of the following describes the purpose of an administration order?

  A   To allow the company to pay its debts before it is liquidated
  B   To prevent legal actions being taken against it
  C   To attempt to rescue the company as a going concern   **(1 mark)**

26.7 Which of the following parties may appoint an administrator without a court order?

  A   A floating chargeholder
  B   A fixed charge holder
  C   An unsecured creditor   **(1 mark)**

26.8 Which of the following names is given to the person in charge of the voluntary winding-up of a company?

  A   Receiver
  B   Chargee
  C   Liquidator
  D   Administrator   **(2 marks)**

26.9 At which point does a members' voluntary winding-up commence?

A   As soon as the members pass the necessary resolution
B   As soon as the Registrar receives a copy of the resolution to wind-up the company
C   As soon as the liquidator is appointed
D   As soon as the directors authorise it after the resolution to wind-up the company is passed

(2 marks)

26.10 Which TWO of the following resolutions may commence a creditors' voluntary winding-up of a company?

(1)   A special resolution of the creditors
(2)   A written resolution of the members with a 75% majority
(3)   A resolution of the board of directors with a 75% majority
(4)   A special resolution of the members

A   1 and 2
B   1 and 4
C   2 and 3
D   2 and 4

(2 marks)

26.11 Which of the following is the title of the liquidator involved in a compulsory liquidation?

A   National receiver
B   Official liquidator
C   Official receiver
D   National liquidator

(2 marks)

26.12 In which publication must the order for a compulsory liquidation be published?

A   The Times
B   The Financial Times
C   The Gazette
D   The Telegraph

(2 marks)

26.13 Which of the following parties has their interest paid first out of a liquidated company's assets?

A   The liquidator
B   Floating chargeholders
C   Employees
D   Those owed deferred debts

(2 marks)

26.14 Which of the following statements concerning administration is correct?

A   A winding-up order may be granted against the company if the company is in administration
B   To commence administration always requires a court order
C   The official receiver is put in charge of a company subject to an administration order
D   If the company cannot be rescued as a going concern, the next objective of administration is to achieve a better result for creditors than an immediate winding-up would

(2 marks)

26.15 Which TWO of the following will end an administration period?

    (1)   After 12 months have elapsed since the administration commenced
    (2)   The success of the administration
    (3)   A court order granted following a special resolution of the members
    (4)   Agreement of the creditors

    A   1 and 2
    B   1 and 4
    C   2 and 3
    D   3 and 4

(2 marks)

(Total = 23 marks)

27.1   Jinx Ltd was formed by two brothers, Son and Lon, who are the company's only shareholders and directors. The company was very successful and has made good profits in every year of trading. However, recently the two brothers have fallen out over some matters in their personal lives and they are no longer talking to each other. This argument, and the resulting lack of trust between Son and Lon, has made running the company almost impossible and business is suffering a consequence.

Son would like to have the company wound-up and is seeking advice.

Required

(a)   State the party that instigates a members' voluntary winding-up and a creditors' voluntary winding up

(2 marks)

(b)   Explain whether Son has grounds to have a court issue an order for the compulsory winding-up of Jinx Ltd.   **(4 marks)**

(Total = 6 marks)

27.2   Aspin is the Finance Director of Getz Ltd. The company has recently gone through a severe downturn in its business and has failed to pay some of its creditors. Six weeks ago, one of the company's creditors, Aero Ltd, made a written demand for the payment of £900. Aspin believes that Getz Ltd may be the subject of a compulsory winding-up order and seeks advice, he is particularly concerned about the effect of a compulsory winding-up on the following matters:

(1)   The sale of a company office building that is currently being advertised
(2)   A threatened legal action by one of Getz Ltd's suppliers against the company
(3)   The company's employees
(4)   A number of floating charges that are secured against company inventory

Required

(a)   State whether Aero Ltd has grounds for the compulsory winding-up of Getz Ltd   **(2 marks)**
(b)   With reference to Aspin's concerns, explain the consequences of compulsory winding-up on Getz Ltd

(4 marks)

(Total = 6 marks)

27.3   Lazy Days Ltd is a coach tour company. It recently leased a fleet of five brand new 'Executive style' coaches ahead of an anticipated increase in business. The coaches cost a total of £20,000 a month to lease, and on top of this, the business also has to pay its overheads including staff costs – a total of £15,000 per month. The increase in business did not materialise and Lazy Days is only generating £28,000 of revenue per month. The coach trips are going out on average 50% full of passengers.

Noelle, the Finance Director is increasingly concerned about the situation and has called a meeting of the board of directors to discuss the matter and the possibility of putting the business into administration.

Required

(a)   State the purpose and effect of an administration order   **(2 marks)**
(b)   Explain the procedure Lazy Days Ltd should follow when appointing an administrator   **(2 marks)**
(c)   Explain whether an administration order would be granted for Lazy Days Ltd   **(2 marks)**

(Total = 6 marks)

27.4 On the advice of his accountant, Mat registered a private limited company to conduct his small manufacturing business. The initial shareholders of the company were Mat, his wife Mary, and her father Norm, who each took 1,000 shares in the company, each with a nominal value of £1. The accountant explained that they did not have to pay the full nominal value of the shares at once, so they each paid only 25p per share taken.

Unfortunately the business has not proved successful and Mat and the other shareholders have decided that it is better to liquidate the company rather than run up any more debts. The current situation is that the company's land is worth £20,000 (secured with a £20,000 loan) and it has further assets to the value of £7,750, but it has debts to business creditors of £10,000 and owes the bank a further £10,000 on its bank overdraft.

Required

(a) State the liability of Mat, Mary and Norm in respect of the company's debts (2 marks)
(b) Explain how the company's debts will be paid out of its liquidated assets (4 marks)
(Total = 6 marks)

27.5 Earl has been employed by Flash Ltd for the past 20 years. During that time, he has also invested in the company in the form of shares and debentures. Earl owns 5,000 ordinary shares in Flash Ltd. The shares are of £1 nominal value and are fully paid-up. The debentures, to the value of £5,000, are secured by a fixed charge against the land on which Flash Ltd's factory is built.

In April it was announced that Flash Ltd was going into immediate insolvent liquidation, owing considerable amounts of money to trade creditors. As a result of the suddenness of the decision to liquidate the company, none of the employees received their last month's wages. In Earl's case this amounted to £2,000.

Required

(a) State whether Earl has any right to his unpaid wages (2 marks)
(b) State the extent of Earl's liability on his share capital (2 marks)
(c) State Earl's rights in respect of his debentures (2 marks)
(Total = 6 marks)

(Total = 30 marks)

28 Fraudulent and criminal behaviour

28.1 In relation to the law on insider dealing, which of the following parties would be categorised as an insider?

   A   A company's auditor
   B   A company's supplier
   C   A company's customer   **(1 mark)**

28.2 Market abuse is an offence under which form of law?

   A   Civil law only
   B   Criminal law only
   C   Civil and criminal law   **(1 mark)**

28.3 In the context of money laundering, the initial disposal of the proceeds of criminal activity is known by which of the following names?

   A   Layering
   B   Integration
   C   Placement   **(1 mark)**

28.4 In the context of money laundering, the transfer of monies in order to disguise their source is known by which of the following names?

   A   Layering
   B   Integration
   C   Placement   **(1 mark)**

28.5 Which of the following statements in relation to the offence of bribery is correct?

   A   Bribery is a tort
   B   Bribery can only be committed in the UK
   C   It is an offence for a corporation to fail to prevent bribery   **(1 mark)**

28.6 Which of the following is the name given to companies that are created by directors of insolvent companies in order to continue their business illegally?

   A   Unicorn companies
   B   Phoenix companies
   C   Dragon companies   **(1 mark)**

28.7 Directors found guilty of fraudulent trading under the Insolvency Act 1986 face which of the following penalties?

   A   Imprisonment
   B   Unlimited fine
   C   Make good the debts of the company   **(1 mark)**

28.8 Which of the following is a defence to a charge of insider dealing?

   A   The individual had no expectation of profit
   B   The individual had reasonable grounds to believe that the information was about to be published
   C   The individual had reasonable grounds to believe their action was in the public interest
   D   The individual was not seeking to profit from the transaction personally   **(2 marks)**

28.9 Which of the following is an example of market abuse?

A An employee who sells shares in their company at a profit
B A finance director who makes a deliberately deceptive profit forecast
C An individual who buys a company's shares on the advice of a broker
D Timing the sale of a company office building so that the sale proceeds are included in the accounts of the current financial year **(2 marks)**

28.10 Which TWO of the following are offences related to money laundering?

(1) Failure to report
(2) Placement
(3) Integration
(4) Tipping off

A 1 and 2
B 1 and 4
C 2 and 3
D 3 and 4 **(2 marks)**

28.11 To whom should a person who suspects another of money laundering report their suspicions to?

A National Crime Agency
B National Audit Office
C Office of Fair trading
D Financial Conduct Authority **(2 marks)**

28.12 Which of the following is NOT classified as bribery under the Bribery Act 2010?

A An individual who accepts payment to perform a public duty
B A company that offers a client reasonable hospitality
C An employee of a company who offers a non-financial reward to a public official to perform a public duty
D A foreign national who works overseas for a company registered in the UK that offers cash to a third party for them to influence a public official **(2 marks)**

28.13 Which of the following must be proved to win a case of fraudulent trading under the Insolvency Act 1986?

A The fraud was due to negligence
B The fraud was intended
C The fraud was profitable
D The fraud was preventable **(2 marks)**

28.14 Which of the following statements concerning wrongful trading is correct?

A Wrongful trading is a criminal offence
B Selling company shares in the knowledge that the share price is about to fall is wrongful trading
C A case of wrongful trading is brought by a company's liquidator
D Intent to defraud is required to prove a case of wrongful trading **(2 marks)**

28.15 Which TWO of the following are offences are connected with the insolvency of a company?

(1) Wrongful trading
(2) Market abuse
(3) Making a false declaration of solvency
(4) Bribery

A   1 and 3
B   1 and 4
C   2 and 3
D   2 and 4

(2 marks)

(Total = 23 marks)

29 MTQ Bank 7

36 mins

29.1 In January the board of directors of Huge plc decided to make a takeover bid for Large plc. After the decision was taken, but before it is announced, the following chain of events occurs:

(1) Slye, a director of Huge plc, buys shares in Large plc
(2) Slye tells his friend Mate about the likelihood of the takeover and Mate buys shares in Large plc
(3) At a dinner party Slye, without actually telling him about the takeover proposal, advises his brother Tim to buy shares in Large plc and Tim does so

Required

(a) State whether Slye committed insider dealing when he bought shares in Large plc **(2 marks)**
(b) State whether Mate has any liability for insider dealing **(2 marks)**
(c) State whether Tim has any liability for insider dealing **(2 marks)**

(Total = 6 marks)

29.2 Five years ago, Del and Rod formed a limited company, Trot Ltd. The pair were the company's only directors and shareholders. The company was initially profitable but started making losses in it's third year. Rod thought that the business should be wound-up at this point but Del persuaded him that the business should continue. Del continued to run the company but Rod, although he retained his position as a director, decided to focus his attention on another business venture.

Trot Ltd continued to make substantial losses, but Del produced fake company accounts to hide the company's debts. Eventually the scale of the losses became to large to hide and the company went into liquidation.

Required

(a) State whether a company must be insolvent for the offence of fraudulent trading to be actionable under the Insolvency Act 1986 and Companies Act 2006 **(2 marks)**
(b) Explain whether Del or Rod will be liable for either:
(i) Fraudulent trading under s213 Insolvency Act 1986
(ii) Wrongful trading under s214 Insolvency Act 1986 **(4 marks)**

(Total = 6 marks)

29.3 Ian is an accountant, and one of his clients is Jet, who runs an illegal operation as well as some other legitimate businesses. Jet approached Ian for advice as to how he should deal with the gains he makes from the illegal operation. Ian suggested that, rather than try to use his existing legitimate businesses to disguise the source of the money, Jet should use his legally made money to buy the local football club, Kickers, with the intention of passing his gains from the illegal operation through the club's accounts.

Jet accepted the proposal and appointed Ian as Kickers' finance director and together they passed the illegal money through the football club.

Required

(a) State the offence of money laundering **(2 marks)**
(b) State whether Ian has any liability for money laundering **(2 marks)**
(c) State whether Jet has any liability for money laundering **(2 marks)**

(Total = 6 marks)

29.4 Sid is a director of two listed public companies in which he has substantial shareholdings: Trend plc and Umber plc.

The annual reports of both Trend plc and Umber plc have just been drawn up, although not yet disclosed. They show that Trend plc has made a surprisingly big loss and that Umber plc has made an equally surprising big profit. On the basis of this information Sid sold his shares in Trend plc and bought shares in Umber plc. He also advised his brother to buy shares in Umber plc.

Vic, who is also a shareholder in both companies, sold a significant number of shares in Umber plc only the day before its annual report was published.

Required

(a) State whether Vic has any right to claim for the increase in share price that he missed out on when he sold his shares **(2 marks)**

(b) Explain any criminal offences Sid may have committed **(4 marks)**

(Total = 6 marks)

29.5 Greg is a member of the board of directors of Huge plc. He also controls a private limited company, Imp Ltd, through which he operates a management consultancy business. He also owns all the shares in Jet Ltd, through which he conducts an investment business.

When Greg learns that Huge plc is going to make a take-over bid for Kop plc, he arranges for Jet Ltd to buy a large number of shares in Kop plc on the London Stock Exchange, on which it makes a large profit when it sells them after the takeover bid is announced. He then arranges for Jet Ltd to transfer the profit to Imp Ltd as the charge for supposed consultancy work. The money is then transferred to Greg through the declaration of dividends by Imp Ltd.

Required

(a) State what is meant by securities being 'price sensitive' in the context of insider dealing **(2 marks)**

(b) State whether Greg has any liability for insider dealing **(2 marks)**

(c) State whether Greg has any liability for money laundering **(2 marks)**

(Total = 6 marks)

(Total = 30 marks)

Answers

1 Law and the legal system

1.1   A   In a criminal law case it is the State that prosecutes the accused.

Syllabus area A1(a)

1.2   B   In a civil law hearing, the claimant must prove their case on the balance of probabilities. Beyond reasonable doubt is the burden of proof in a criminal law hearing.

Syllabus area A1(a)

1.3   C   Damages is a remedy under civil law. Fines and imprisonment are only available under criminal law.

Syllabus area A1(a)

1.4   B   All criminal cases begin in a Magistrate's Court.

Syllabus area A1(b)

1.5   C   The Queen's Bench, Family and Chancery are all divisions of the High Court.

Syllabus area A1(b)

1.6   A   In a Magistrate's Court, cases are decided by the Magistrate because there is no jury. The Magistrate's Court does have some civil jurisdiction, for example in family proceedings. Appeals are usually made to the Crown Court, but the High Court may also hear them.

Syllabus area A1(b)

1.7   B   Summary offences are minor offences that would only be heard at a Magistrate's Court. Indictable offences are serious offences that would only be heard at a Crown Court. A 'triable either way' offence is one where the accused has the choice of which court will hear the case.

Syllabus area A1(b)

1.8   A   Public law is concerned with the operation of the Government and public organisations such as Councils and Local Authorities.

Syllabus area A1(a)

1.9   A   Criminal law is a form of public law and is associated with punishment. Civil law is private law and is associated with compensation. In a civil law case a claimant sues a defendant. In criminal law the parties are the accused and prosecution.

Syllabus area A1(a)

1.10   C   A civil law case is between the claimant and defendant. A criminal law case is between the prosecution and accused.

Syllabus area A1(a)

1.11   B   In the civil law system, cases are allocated to either the 'fast', 'small' or 'multi' track depending on the size and complexity of the claim.

Syllabus area A1(b)

1.12   B   In the criminal law system, an appeal regarding a decision by a Magistrate's Court would be heard by the Crown Court. Appeals can also be made by way of case stated to the Divisional Court of Queen's Bench in the High Court, but this was not one of the options.

Syllabus area A1(b)

1.13   A   It is the County Court that only has civil jurisdiction.

Syllabus area A1(b)

1.14   B   The Chancery Division would deal with matters relating to trusts and mortgages. Contract law cases would be heard by the Queen's Bench Division. Matrimonial cases and proceedings involving children (such as adoption) would be heard by the Family Division.

Syllabus area A1(b)

1.15   C   A Magistrate's Court hears minor, summary, offences without a jury. A Crown Court hears serious, indictable, offences with a jury. Some offences are 'triable either way' and can be heard at either a Magistrate's or Crown Court. The is no such offence as a 'hybrid' offence.

Syllabus area A1(b)

2 Sources of law

2.1   C   It is the ratio decidendi that becomes binding on future judges. Obiter dicta are statements said 'by the way' and are not binding. Per incuriam is a legal term that means 'made without care'.

Syllabus area A2(a)

2.2   A   A reversing decision is made when a case is appealed. An overruling decision occurs when a superior court overturns the decision of a lower court in a different case. Distinguishing occurs when a judge decides not to follow a precedent in the case before them because the material facts of the two cases are sufficiently different.

Syllabus area A2(a)

2.3   A   Parliamentary sovereignty means that Parliament may modify or replace existing statutes. Legislation may overrule or modify existing case law but may not prevent a future Parliament from changing the law.

Syllabus area A2(b)

2.4   C   Private Acts affect specific individuals or groups. Public Acts affect the general public. Enabling legislation empowers a specific individual or body to produce the detail required by a parent Act.

Syllabus area A2(b)

2.5   A   The golden rule states that words in a statute should be given their plain, ordinary meaning unless this would give rise to a manifest absurdity or inconsistency with the rest of the statute. The mischief rule states that judges should consider what mischief the Act was trying to prevent. The contextual rule states that a word should be construed in its context.

Syllabus area A2(c)

2.6   B   The long title is an element of the Act and is therefore an intrinsic aid. Hansard and Law Commission reports are not part of the Act and are therefore extrinsic aids.

Syllabus area A2(c)

2.7   B   The European Court of Human Rights is the final appeal court for human rights issues in the UK.

Syllabus area A2(d)

2.8   D   The only courts that bind the Court of Appeal are the Supreme Court, the European Court of Justice and itself.

Syllabus area A2(a)

2.9   A   Mistakes by judges can never be eliminated. The other options are correct statements concerning binding precedent.

Syllabus area A2(a)

2.10   A   The stages that a Bill passes through before becoming legislation are: First reading, second reading, committee stage, report stage, third reading, pass through same stages in the other House and Royal Assent.

Syllabus area A2(b)

2.11   D   Statutory instruments must be laid before Parliament for 40 days before coming into effect.

Syllabus area A2(b)

2.12   C   Under the purposive approach to statutory interpretation, the purpose, or what the legislation is trying to achieve, is considered.

Syllabus area A2(c)

2.13   B   A statute does not have retrospective effect. However, a person may be deprived of their property (but they must be compensated for this), the Crown is not bound by statute and statutes only have effect in the UK.

Syllabus area A2(c)

2.14   A   Extrinsic aids do not form part of the Act. Hansard is an example of an extrinsic aid.

Syllabus area A2(c)

2.15   C   Under the Human Rights Act 1998 courts may strike out secondary legislation that is incompatible with the Convention and must interpret legislation in such a way that is compatible with it. New legislation does not have to be compatible with the Convention, but a statement to that effect must be made before the Bill becomes law. Under the Human Rights Act 1998, UK courts must take the decisions of the European Court of Justice into account when making judgements.

Syllabus area A2(d)

3 Formation of contract I

3.1   A   A conveyance must be in the form of a deed. A transfer of shares and a consumer credit contract must be in writing.

Syllabus area B1(a)

3.2   C   An offer is defined as a promise to be bound on specific terms and can be made in any form such as in writing or verbally. A statement of possible terms is a supply of information. Displaying goods for sale is an invitation to treat.

Syllabus area B1(b)

3.3   B   In a sale by auction that is stated to be 'without reserve', the auctioneer presenting the goods for sale is the offer and a bid represents acceptance.

Syllabus area B1(b)

3.4   C   If no time period is set for its expiry, an offer will remain open for a reasonable time. What is reasonable will depend on the circumstances.

Syllabus area B1(c)

3.5   C   The death of the offeree will terminate an offer. Posting a letter of revocation is not sufficient to terminate an offer, it must be received before acceptance is made in order to be effective. A request for information will also not terminate an offer.

Syllabus area B1(c)

3.6   C   Acceptance may be made by express words or conduct of the offeree. Silence is not valid acceptance.

Syllabus area B1(d)

3.7   B   The postal rule states that acceptance is effective once the letter of acceptance is posted.

Syllabus area B1(d)

3.8   C   A standard form contract is a document set out by large organisations that states the terms that its customers will do business with it. There is no negotiation, either the customer accepts the terms or goes elsewhere. The contracts in the other options include scope for negotiation.

Syllabus area B1(a)

3.9 B The law may interfere in the formation of contracts, but only to ensure that stronger parties do not abuse their position. The law does not seek to maintain or amend bargaining power.

Syllabus area B1(a)

3.10 B An offer is a definite promise to be bound on specific terms and can be made in a number of forms. Therefore a verbal statement to sell something to another person is an offer. Newspaper adverts and price lists are examples of invitations to treat. At a supermarket checkout, the person handing their goods to the checkout operator is making an offer to buy the goods.

Syllabus area B1(b)

3.11 C Although newspaper adverts are usually considered invitations to treat, they will be regarded as offers if they are made to the world at large and are sufficiently specific. The other options are examples of invitations to treat.

Syllabus area B1(b)

3.12 A Counter-offers have the effect of terminating the original offer, but may be accepted by the original offeror. A statement that enquiries whether alternative terms would be acceptable is a request for information, not a counter-offer. Counter-offers are made by the original offeree to the original offeror.

Syllabus area B1(c)

3.13 B A third party who is sufficiently reliable may reject an offer on behalf of the offeree. Letters of revocation are only effective when they are received by the offeree, not when they are posted. Enquiring whether another method of payment would be acceptable is a request for information that does not terminate the original offer. The death of the offeror does not terminate the offer is the offeree is unaware of the death and the contract is not of a personal nature.

Syllabus area B1(c)

3.14 D The postal rule states that acceptance is valid when a letter of acceptance is posted. The other options are not regarded as acceptance – a counter-offer is in effect a new offer, acceptance 'subject to contract' means the offeree is agreeable to the terms but the parties should negotiate a valid contract, and a tender to perform a task is an offer.

Syllabus area B1(d)

3.15 B A unilateral contract is one where there is a promise to pay money in return for an act – such as an offer to pay a reward for the return of an item. In such cases, acceptance does not need to be communicated because a contract is formed when the item is returned. Under the postal rule, a letter of acceptance just needs to be posted for acceptance to be valid. If two identical offers cross in the post then there is no contract – just two offers. Where no method of communication of acceptance is required then any method of acceptance can be used.

Syllabus area B1(d)

4 Formation of contract II

4.1 A Executed consideration takes place at the same time. Executory consideration takes place at a future date. Past consideration is something that has already been done.

Syllabus area B1(e)

4.2 C Courts will not interfere in contracts in regards to the adequacy of consideration.

Syllabus area B1(f)

4.3 B Consideration must be sufficient but not necessarily adequate. It must have some economic value to be sufficient.

Syllabus area B1(f)

4.4　B　Privity of contract means that only parties to a contract have enforceable rights under it. The concept applies to both rights and obligations under a contract. Generally, third parties do not have enforceable rights under a contract.

Syllabus area B1(g)

4.5　C　Two exceptions to the rule of privity of contract are that a third party can sue for foreseeable losses they incur and if an implied trust has been created.

Syllabus area B1(g)

4.6　C　The presumption is that social arrangements are not intended to be legally binding and commercial arrangements are intended to be legally binding. However, this presumption is rebuttable and a contract will be legally binding if both parties intended it to be so.

Syllabus area B1(h)

4.7　B　The courts are very ready to impute an intention to be legally bound where a husband and wife agree to transfer property between them. Letters of comfort and transactions 'binding in honour only' both indicate there is no intention to be legally bound.

Syllabus area B1(h)

4.8　A　Consideration must pass from the promisee. It must be sufficient but not necessarily adequate. Past consideration is generally not valid consideration. Executory consideration is generally valid consideration.

Syllabus area B1(e)

4.9　A　Past consideration is sufficient to create liability on a bill of exchange – this is one of the few exceptions to the rule on past consideration. Suffering loss or detriment is valid consideration. Impossible or illegal acts are not valid consideration.

Syllabus area B1(e)

4.10　A　For the extra consideration to be valid, the creditor must become entitled to something that they are not already entitled to. In this case, goods rather than cash and payment by a third party are valid examples. A guarantee of payment and payment on time are not valid as extra consideration because the creditor is already entitled to them.

Syllabus area B1(f)

4.11　C　The performance of an existing contractual duty is not sufficient consideration for the promise of additional reward unless an additional service is also provided, or if the duty is provided to a third party instead.

Syllabus area B1(f)

4.12　A　Privity of contract means that only parties to a contract may sue on it. The Contracts (Rights of Third Parties) Act 1999 is a source of regulation. There are exceptions to the rule of privity. Privity of contract applies to all contracts, not just commercial ones.

Syllabus area B1(g)

4.13　B　Third parties need not have been in existence when the contract was formed but must be expressly identified in the contract. The Act does not confer rights to third parties in respect of a company's constitution or employment contracts.

Syllabus area B1(g)

4.14　D　Parties in social, domestic and family agreements are presumed not to intend to be legally bound, but this presumption is rebuttable. Parties in commercial contracts are presumed to intend to be legally bound but this presumption is rebuttable. With regard to rebutting either presumption, the burden of proof is on the party seeking to escape liability.

Syllabus area B1(h)

4.15 C Agreements from a husband and wife who have separated, and between friends who have entered a competition, have both been held by the courts as legally binding agreements. Payment of a monthly allowance and housekeeping money are not viewed as intending to be legally binding.

Syllabus area B1(h)

5 Content of contracts

5.1 A Where a term of a contract is found to be untrue then the party can sue for breach of contract. A party can sue for misrepresentation when a representation (which is not a term) proves to be untrue.

Syllabus area B2(a)

5.2 A A representation is something said before a contract is formed, that induces the formation of the contract, but does not become a term of the contract.

Syllabus area B2(a)

5.3 A Terms can be implied into contracts by statute (for example the Sale of Goods Act 1979). The courts may imply terms into contracts in order to give the contract efficacy. Express terms will override terms implied by custom.

Syllabus area B2(b)

5.4 B A warranty is a term subsidiary to the main purpose of the contract, that, if breached, entitles the injured party to claim damages. A condition is a term vital to the contract. An implied term is a term that is not expressly stated by the parties.

Syllabus area B2(b)

5.5 C Particularly unusual or onerous terms must be highlighted. Previous consistent dealings can be enough to incorporate terms into a contract. A person is deemed to have read a contract if they have signed it.

Syllabus area B2(c)

5.6 B The contra proferentem rule states that any ambiguity in exclusion clauses is to be interpreted against the person seeking to rely on them.

Syllabus area B2(c)

5.7 A The main purpose rule states that the purpose of an exclusion clause is not to prevent the main purpose of the contract.

Syllabus area B2(c)

5.8 B A representation is something that induces the formation of a contract but does not become a term of a contract. They are made during pre-contract negotiations.

Syllabus area B2(a)

5.9 C Express terms are expressly agreed by the parties. The other options are examples of how terms are implied into contracts.

Syllabus area B2(b)

5.10 A The principle of freedom of contracts states that parties are generally free to form a contract as they wish, but to be valid, a contract must be complete in its terms. Parties may include a term that allows a third party to determine an essential term. Where a condition is breached, the injured party may claim damages or treat the contract as discharged.

Syllabus area B2(b)

5.11 C The classification of an innominate term is determined by the courts.

Syllabus area B2(b)

5.12   B   Exclusion clauses are interpreted by the courts strictly. They must be incorporated before the contract is formed and are regulated by statute law. Exclusion clauses may exclude liability for negligence but not for death or injury due to negligence.

Syllabus area B2(c)

5.13   A   Under s5 UCTA 1977, a guarantee clause that seeks to exclude liability for loss or damage caused by a defect in a consumer good is void. UCTA 1977 does not apply to contracts of insurance. In commercial contracts, parties may exclude liability for loss or damage caused by negligence and breach of contract.

Syllabus area B2(c)

5.14   A   As its name suggests, UTCCR 1999 only applies to consumer contracts. A consumer must be a natural person who is not acting in the course of their business. The regulations only apply to terms that have not been individually negotiated.

Syllabus area B2(c)

5.15   C   The Unfair Contract Terms Act 1977 applies to consumer and commercial contracts and to all terms, whether individually negotiated or not. A company may be classed as a consumer if the contract is incidental to its business. In a commercial contract, terms which seek to restrict liability for loss or damage (other than injury or death) caused by negligence are not automatically void, they are subject to a reasonableness test.

Syllabus area B2(c)

6 Breach of contract and remedies

6.1   C   Performance which is impossible is a legal excuse for non-performance, as is agreement. Financial hardship is not a lawful excuse for non-performance.

Syllabus area B3(a)

6.2   B   Anticipatory breach of contract occurs where one party states before the time of performance that they will not perform their obligations.

Syllabus area B3(b)

6.3   A   Renunciation involves one party stating they have no intention of performing their obligations. Incapacitation involves one party preventing themselves from performing their obligations. Frustration is occurs where external circumstances prevent a party from performing their obligations.

Syllabus area B3(b)

6.4   B   Damages paid to protect reliance interest recover what the claimant has lost due to relying on the contract. Damages paid to put the claimant into the position they would have been in if the contract was performed protect expectation interest. Action for the price is a common law remedy to recover the price of goods or services provided.

Syllabus area B3(c)

6.5   A   Liquidated damages is a genuine pre-estimate of losses payable in the event of a breach of contract. A penalty clause is a fixed amount payable on breach of contract.

Syllabus area B3(c)

6.6   C   Specific performance is typically awarded in contracts for the sale of property. It is not made in respect of contracts for employment or personal services.

Syllabus area B3(d)

6.7   A   An injunction is an equitable remedy. Action for the price and quantum meruit are common law remedies.

Syllabus area B3(d)

6.8   D   In the event of repudiatory breach, the innocent party may affirm the contract and continue with their obligations. They must inform the other party if they intend to terminate the contract. They may claim damages or treat the contract as discharged. They can refuse to pay for partial or defective performance already received.

Syllabus area B3(b)

6.9   C   Just because performance is more expensive than agreed does not mean the party does not have to perform their obligations. The other options are lawful reasons for non-performance.

Syllabus area B3(b)

6.10   D   To be claimable, losses must arise naturally from the breach of contract. If they arise outside the normal course of events, the circumstances must be within the defendant's knowledge when they made the contract.

Syllabus area B3(c)

6.11   C   Innocent parties are required to mitigate their losses. Damages are payable in respect of mental distress – although the scope of such payments is limited. Damages that are wholly disproportionate to the breach are not payable *(Ruxley Electronics and Construction Ltd v Forsyth 1995)*. Penalty clauses are void and not enforceable.

Syllabus area B3(c)

6.12   B   Liquidated damage clauses are onerous terms that must be highlighted in the contract. They are valid and enforceable. Their purpose is to compensate the innocent party for losses incurred, not to deter breaches of contract. They are payable where conditions, warranties and innominate terms are breached.

Syllabus area B3(c)

6.13   C   Injunctions require a defendant to observe negative restrictions of a contract. They are an equitable remedy that are awarded when damages are inadequate compensation. The award of an injunction is entirely at the discretion of the court.

Syllabus area B3(d)

6.14   D   For an award of rescission to be made, innocent third parties must not have acquired rights under the subject matter of the contract. Both parties must be able to be restored to their pre-contract position. The right to rescind must be exercised within a reasonable time of it being awarded. The right to rescind expires if the contract is affirmed.

Syllabus area B3(d)

6.15   A   For an order of specific performance to be made, damages must be an inadequate remedy and consideration must have passed. Both parties do not have to agree to the remedy and it will not be awarded when the contract requires performance over a long period of time.

Syllabus area B3(d)

7 The law of torts and professional negligence

7.1   C   Torts are civil wrongs, not crimes or breaches of contract, and the victim sues for compensation or an injunction.

Syllabus area B4(a)

7.2   A   'Passing-off' is the use of a business name or trademark that misleads a consumer to believe that a business is that of another.

Syllabus area B4(b)

| 7.3 | B | For the defendant to be liable in negligence, the claimant must prove that the defendant had a duty to avoid causing them loss, injury or damage, that the defendant breached that duty, and as a consequence of the breach, the claimant suffered loss, injury or damage. |

Syllabus area B4(c)

| 7.4 | B | Where res ipsa loquitur applies, the burden of proof is reversed and the defendant must prove that they were not negligent. |

Syllabus area B4(c)

| 7.5 | A | In the tort of negligence, pure economic loss is usually not recoverable. |

Syllabus area B4(d)

| 7.6 | B | Volenti non fit injuria means the claimant voluntarily accepted the risk of injury and the defendant is not liable. |

Syllabus area B4(e)

| 7.7 | C | Following the *Caparo* decision, a company's auditors do not owe a duty of care to the public at large or to shareholders increasing their stakes. They only owe a duty of care to the company. |

Syllabus area B4(f)

| 7.8 | B | In tort, no contractual relationship need exist between claimant and defendant. A number of remedies are available to a victim of a tort, such as an injunction or compensation. Torts are heard in the civil court system. The burden of proof is generally on the claimant unless res ipsa loquitur is established. |

Syllabus area B4(a)

| 7.9 | C | 'Passing-off' involves the use of a business name, trademark or description that is similar enough to another business so that the consumer is misled to believe that one business is that of another. |

Syllabus area B4(b)

| 7.10 | D | The three questions that must be asked to establish a duty of care are: Was the harm reasonably foreseeable?, Was there a relationship of proximity between the parties?, and is it fair, just and reasonable to impose a duty of care? |

Syllabus area B4(c)

| 7.11 | C | Defendants are not expected to take precautions if the cost or disruption caused outweighs the risk. Where there is a high probability of injury the defendant should take extra care. Social benefit of a defendant's actions may protect them from liability. A professional is expected to show the same level of skill as a reasonable person possessing the same skill. |

Syllabus area B4(c)

| 7.12 | D | Where there are multiple possible causes, the court must establish that the negligent act was the one that caused the injury. If this is not possible then causality is not established. The other options are examples of circumstances that will not prevent causality being established. |

Syllabus area B4(d)

| 7.13 | D | Reductions for contributory negligence are typically in the range of 10% to 75%, but it is possible to reduce the claim by 100% *(Jayes v IMI (Kynoch) Ltd 1985)*. |

Syllabus area B4(e)

| 7.14 | B | Following the *Caparo* decision, the accountants do not owe a duty of care to the shareholders or the general public. There is no special relationship with the bidding company so no duty of care is owed to that. Following the case of *Morgan Crucible Co plc v Hill Samuel Ltd and others 1991*, the accountants owe a higher standard of care to the target company because the report will be used in a take-over bid. |

Syllabus area B4(f)

7.15 B   Following the *Caparo* decision, the auditors do not owe a duty of care to the shareholders of the parent company. There is no special relationship with the rival company, so no duty of care is owed to that. Following the cases of *Barings plc and Cooper & Lybrand 1997* and *BCCI (Overseas) Ltd v Ernst & Whinney 1997*, the auditors of a subsidiary company owe a duty of the care to both the parent and subsidiary companies.

Syllabus area B4(f)

8 MTQ Bank 1

8.1

Text reference. Chapter 3.

Top tips. This scenario question is typical of the type of question you must expect in the exam. It requires you to analyse the scenario and apply principles of contract law to it. You must not expect there to be one simple and obvious answer to a question like this. Comparing this situation to case law that you are aware of will help you identify what is most likely to be the case here.

(a)   An offer is a definite promise to be bound on specific terms. It must be certain in its terms and can be made to a particular person or to a class of persons. An invitation to treat is an indication that a person is prepared to receive offers with a view to entering into a binding contract. It is generally accepted that goods displayed in a shop window give rise to an invitation to treat rather than an offer *(Fisher v Bell 1961)*. Therefore, the notice in Ann's window is almost certainly an invitation to treat.

(b)   Because the parties negotiated face-to-face it is likely that the use of the post is outside the contemplation of the parties and therefore any acceptance should not be by post. However, Chas' acceptance arrived within the stipulated time and therefore an enforceable contract for sale exists from this point.

(c)   It is probable that Dave, however, has not entered into an enforceable contract for sale with Ann because his acceptance was not communicated by noon on Monday and the postal rule was not in the reasonable contemplation of the parties.

8.2

Text reference. Chapter 3.

Top tips. Explaining the *Carlill* case is important to demonstrate an understanding of how the law works, but you could have explained the law without reference to this case.

(a)   In a unilateral contract, the party whose performance is sought is not obligated to act, but if they do, the offeror is bound to comply with the terms of the agreement. In a bilateral contract both parties are bound by an exchange of promises. The offer of a reward for some kind of performance is therefore a unilateral contract.

(b)   The terms of Ace Ltd's offer clearly state that it is open to employees of Ace Ltd only. In general, offers can be made to the world at large, but where they are addressed to a specific group of people then only those within that group can accept them. Therefore Cid has no right to claim anything from Ace Ltd.

(c)   Usually an offeror may revoke their offer at any time before acceptance *(Routledge v Grant 1828)*. However this is not the case in unilateral contracts and revocation is not possible once the offeree has begun to perform the task specified in the offer *(Errington v Errington 1953)*. Ed is an employee and therefore included in the terms of the offer. Ace Ltd is not permitted to revoke the offer and therefore since he solved the problem before the deadline Ed is entitled to the reward.

8.3

> **Text reference**. Chapter 4.
>
> **Top tips**. You must be very clear in your mind about what the issue is before starting to write. It is easy to misinterpret this question so make sure you focus on what's important – the need for consideration to support a promise to waive a debt.

(a) Zri's agreement to accept only half of the debt is unsupported by consideration from Ad and therefore he may still claim the remaining amount. Ad may try to claim he cannot do so because of his promise to waive the fees and therefore the doctrine of promissory estoppel applies. However, it does not appear from the scenario that Ad relied on the promise so the doctrine would not apply and Zri should be able to recover the remaining debt from him.

(b) (i) In general, where a party pays less than the amount due, the person who is owed the money is entitled to claim full payment at a later date. However, this rule does not apply where consideration is provided to support this promise.

Zri agreed to accept accountancy work from Bi as a payment in kind, and payment in another form is valid consideration for a promise to waive part of a debt *(Anon 1495)*. Zri therefore may not recover any further sum from Bi *(Anon 1495)*.

(ii) Although Zri accepted part-payment from Cas, the part-payment came from a third party, and payment from a third party is valid consideration to waive a debt *(Welby v Drake 1825)*. Zri therefore cannot enforce the remainder of the debt.

8.4

> **Text reference**. Chapter 5.
>
> **Top tips**. Read the question carefully. Highlight the question paper for key points or annotate the margin. Make sure that you identify the issues involved and are fully familiar with the scenario before you start your answer.

(a) An exclusion or exemption clause, can be defined as 'a clause in a contract which purports to exclude liability altogether or to restrict it by limiting damages or by imposing other onerous conditions'.

(b) The Unfair Contract Terms Act 1977 divides exclusion clauses into two types; those that are void and those that are valid only as far as they are reasonable. Under s2, liability for personal injury or death due to negligence may never be excluded. An exemption for loss due to negligence in other circumstances will be valid only insofar as it is reasonable. Reasonableness is to be considered with reference to the parties' obligations of skill and care.

(i) The exclusion clause seeking to exempt Bash Ltd from liability for the damage to Andy's car will only be valid if it is reasonable. Courts will take into account all the circumstances that were known, or ought to have been known by the parties when the contract was made and it will be up to Bash Ltd to prove that the clause was reasonable: *St Albans City and District Council v International Computers Ltd 1994.* The company would be unlikely to succeed in avoiding liability for damage to Andy's car since it is reasonable to expect its driver not to be negligent in operating such a tow vehicle. Andy can claim damages.

(ii) Taking into account s2 of UCTA 1977, Bash Ltd would not be able to rely on the exclusion clause to avoid liability for the injuries to Andy that arose from its negligence due to the actions of the towing vehicle's driver. Andy can claim damages.

8.5

Text reference. Chapter 7.

Top tips. There are two defences to a negligence claim and this question tests both. Ensure you learn them!

(a)   To establish a duty of care, a claimant must prove that the harm was reasonably foreseeable, there was a relationship of proximity between the parties and it is fair, just and reasonable to impose a duty of care.

(b)   Volenti non fit injuria is the voluntary acceptance of the risk of injury and is a defence to a claim of negligence. It applies where the claimant expressly consented to the risk (such as on waiver forms signed by those taking part in dangerous sports), or it may be implied by their conduct.

Whilst it is not clear that Roger expressly agreed to the risk, it is reasonable for him to expect it. Roger has taken part in many fights, so he cannot argue that he was not aware of the risk – therefore the organisers are likely to be exonerated from any liability under negligence for the injuries caused to Roger.

(c)   Contributory negligence does not exonerate the defendant from their negligence completely, but their liability to pay compensation may be reduced by the courts if the injured party is proved to have contributed to the loss they suffered in some way. In the case of *Sayers v Harlow UDC 1958*, a lady was injured while trying to climb out of a public toilet cubicle which had a defective lock. The court held that she had contributed to her injuries by the method by which she had tried to climb out.

This case is almost identical to Lulu's so it is expected that the train station may use this defence and the courts will reduce damages awarded to Lulu on a percentage basis that is just and reasonable. This is typically in the range of 10% to 75%, however it is possible to reduce the claim by up to 100%.

9 Contract of employment

9.1   A   An employee works under a contract of service. A self-employed person works under a contract for services.

Syllabus area C1(a)

9.2   A   Ownership of tools is a classic example of an indication of being self-employed. The other options indicate that the person is an employee.

Syllabus area C1(a)

9.3   B   The self-employed can register and charge VAT on their services. The other options are consequences of being an employee.

Syllabus area C1(a)

9.4   C   Employment contracts may be oral or in writing. As with all contracts, consideration is required. Terms can be implied from trade custom and practice.

Syllabus area C1(b)

9.5   C   Reasonable care and skill is a common law duty of an employee. Employees do not have to obey all instructions (for example they can refuse to put their health and safety at risk). They have a duty of reasonable competence, but this does not refer to qualifications.

Syllabus area C1(b)

9.6   B   Providing health insurance is not a common law duty of an employer. The other options are common law duties.

Syllabus area C1(b)

9.7   C   Trade union officials are entitled to time off on full pay to carry out trade union duties. Trade union members are entitled to time off to attend trade union meetings but there is no right to pay.

Syllabus area C1(b)

9.8 B   The integration test asks whether the person is so skilled that they cannot be controlled in the performance of their duties. Lack of control indicates the person is not integrated into the employer's organisation. The control test considers whether the employer has control over the way the employee performs their duties. The multiple (economic reality) test considers whether the employee works on their own account.

Syllabus area C1(a)

9.9 C   The provision of work tools by an employer is a sign that the person is an employee. The other options indicate the person is self-employed.

Syllabus area C1(a)

9.10 C   Vicarious liability and the deduction of PAYE tax are consequences of being an employee. The other options are consequences of being self-employed.

Syllabus area C1(a)

9.11 B   The self-employed are not entitled to a minimum notice period.

Syllabus area C1(a)

9.12 B   The written statement of prescribed particulars must be provided within two months following the commencement of employment.

Syllabus area C1(b)

9.13 D   There is no right to workplace childcare.

Syllabus area C1(b)

9.14 D   An employer may reasonably refuse a request for flexible working.

Syllabus area C1(b)

9.15 A   Employees are entitled to an itemised pay slip and a minimum hourly wage rate. Parental leave is available but it is unpaid. Under the Working Time Regulations 1998, an employee's hours in a 17-week block should not exceed 48 hours in each 7 day period.

Syllabus area C1(b)

10 Dismissal and redundancy

10.1 C   Employees with between two and ten years of continuous service are entitled to one week's notice for every year of employment.

Syllabus area C2(a)

10.2 B   Dismissal without notice is known as summary dismissal.

Syllabus area C2(b)

10.3 C   Wrongful dismissal occurs when an employee is summarily dismissed without justification. This means they did not receive the correct notice period. A claim for wrongful dismissal seeks compensation for the loss of notice period.

Syllabus area C2(c)

10.4 A   Damages for wrongful dismissal are to recover lost earnings. They do not include an amount for mental distress and wrongful dismissal is not a criminal offence.

Syllabus area C2(c)

10.5 A   An employee who is pregnant is exempt from the need to have a minimum period of continuous service before being able to claim unfair dismissal.

Syllabus area C2(d)

10.6 B A basic award is subject to a statutory maximum but is based on the employee's age, pay and length of service. A compensatory award is subject to a statutory maximum. Additional awards are only granted where the employer does not comply with an order for reinstatement or re-engagement.

Syllabus area C2(e)

10.7 C An employee must have a minimum of two years' continuous service before being entitled to redundancy pay.

Syllabus area C2(f)

10.8 A An employee who has been continuously employed for over a month must give a minimum of one week's notice to their employer if they decide to leave.

Syllabus area C2(a)

10.9 C Constructive dismissal occurs where the employer resigns following their employer's breach of contract. Dismissal without correct notice and justification is wrongful dismissal. Dismissal without notice is summary dismissal.

Syllabus area C2(b)

10.10 A Only serious misbehaviour by the employee will justify summary dismissal. Misconduct and gross negligence are serious reasons. Lateness and failure to follow a dress code are unlikely to warrant summary dismissal.

Syllabus area C2(c)

10.11 A Wrongful dismissal involves a breach of contract and damages are payable for the loss of notice period only. The other remedies are for unfair dismissal.

Syllabus area C2(c)

10.12 A The resignation of an employee does not count as dismissal in an unfair dismissal case. The other options are examples of dismissal for unfair dismissal purposes.

Syllabus area C2(d)

10.13 C Capability or qualifications is a fair reason for dismissal. The other options are unfair reasons for dismissal.

Syllabus area C2(d)

10.14 B Compensation for unfair dismissal is a statutory concept, not just based on common law principles relating to breach of contract. It will not be reduced just because it may exceed lost earnings. The other options are circumstances where an award may be reduced.

Syllabus area C2(e)

10.15 B Employees who were or could have been dismissed before the redundancy notice cannot claim a redundancy payment. An employee who unreasonably refuses a renewal to their contract cannot claim a redundancy payment. A claim can be made within six months and those involved in strike action after the redundancy notice can claim a redundancy payment.

Syllabus area C2(f)

11 MTQ Bank 2

11.1

(a) The issue regarding the 'professionals' is their integration with the company. Using the integration test, the courts consider whether the employee is so skilled that they cannot be controlled in the performance of their duties. In *Cassidy v Ministry of Health 1951* a doctor was held to be an employee as they were selected for a particular task and integrated into the organisation to perform certain surgical operations. If patients had the right to choose the doctor, this would indicate that the doctor was not so integrated and they would have been treated as an independent contractor. It is therefore likely that the 'professionals' will be classified as independent contractors.

(b) The issue regarding the 'techies' is the degree of control the company has over them. Using the control test, a court will consider whether the employer has control over the way in which the employee performs their duties. Where it appears that the 'employer' may control how the 'employee's' duties are performed, then they will be treated as an employee; *Mersey Docks & Harbour Board v Coggins & Griffiths (Liverpool) 1947*. Gem Ltd has very little control over how the 'techies' do their work and therefore they will be classified as independent contractors.

(c) Using the economic reality (multiple) test, courts focus on whether the 'employee' was working on their own account and this requires numerous factors to be considered. One of these factors is whether it is the employee or employer who provides work tools. Because Gem Ltd provides the 'greasemonkees' tools, they will be considered as employees.

11.2

(a) Constructive dismissal takes place where the employer repudiates some vital term of the employment contract and, despite the employer's willingness to continue the employment, the employee resigns because of it. No notice of termination is served on either party. In such cases, the employer is liable for breach of contract and unfair dismissal.

(b) Unilaterally imposing a complete change in the employee's duties or reducing the employee's pay have been held to be sufficiently serious to entitle the employee to claim breach of contract and claim for constructive dismissal.

(c) Fine Ltd has repudiated a vital term of Gus's contract (location) and Gus resigned because of it. There appears to be no mobility clause in Gus's contract that would require him to relocate. Therefore Fine Ltd has constructively dismissed Gus and he can therefore claim compensation for unfair dismissal.

11.3

(a) Grace has been dismissed because her employer has closed her shop and therefore no longer requires a shop manager. This means that it has ceased carrying on the business in which the Grace has been employed and therefore Grace has been made redundant.

(b) An employer may choose to offer a redundant employee alternative employment. If the employee unreasonably refuses the offer, they lose their entitlement to a redundancy payment. Broadly speaking, the alternative employment must be in the same capacity, at the same place and on the same terms and conditions as the old employment. It should not be perceived as being lower in status.

(c)   Grace has been employed for three years and is 33 years old. According the rules of statutory redundancy pay she is entitled to a redundancy payment of one week's pay per complete year of employment. She will therefore receive three weeks' pay (although a week's pay is subject to a statutory maximum).

11.4

> **Text reference**. Chapters 10 and 11.
>
> **Top tips**. You must learn the tests of employment.

(a)   The distinction between employees and independent contractors depends on many factors. The courts will primarily look at the reality of the situation rather than accept the form of the arrangement at face value. Initially, they will look at the relationship between the parties and any agreement between them. Where the 'employee's' status is still unclear, a series of tests will be applied; the control, integration and economic reality (multiple) tests.

(b)   Using the three tests it would appear that Fred is self-employed. The main reason for this is the fact that Dan has little control over Fred's work. For example, he can work at home, on other projects and even delegate his work to others if he so decides. As self-employed, Fred has no rights with regard to his loss of work and may not claim any payment or compensation from Dan.

(c)   Using the same tests it would appear that Eve is an employee. This is because Dan exercises sufficient control over her work, for example by not allowing her to take on other work and requiring her to attend his premises every day. As an employee, Eve has the right to claim redundancy because her services are no longer required by Dan. She will be able to claim a redundancy payment, calculated using the rules already discussed.

11.5

> **Text reference**. Chapter 9.
>
> **Top tips**. When reading through the question, make sure that you pick up all the details that might be relevant to your answer. For example, you are told that the staff members have been employed for six years, so you do not need to discuss factors such as the time requirements for actions for unfair dismissal.

(a)   When a case comes before an employment tribunal it is for the employer to prove that the dismissal was for a fair reason (capability, conduct, redundancy, legal prohibition or another substantial reason). However, there are automatically unfair reasons for dismissal that the employee might raise, and in that case the employer should be prepared to defend against them. In cases of redundancy, a fair selection process should be used to select employees for dismissal.

(b)   Fred feels that his confrontations with Jack are related to an automatically unfair reason for dismissal (trade union membership), and this is why he was dismissed. However, he will need to prove this to any employment tribunal.

(c)   Gale's position is a little more straightforward. She is pregnant and she has been dismissed. Pregnancy is an automatically unfair reason for dismissal that cannot be disputed. Therefore it is likely that she will succeed in proving that she was dismissed unfairly.

12 Agency law

12.1   C   In an agency relationship, the purpose of the agent is to form a contract between the principal and a third party.

Syllabus area D1(a)

12.2   C   Express agreements can be oral or in writing.

Syllabus area D1(b)

12.3   B   Agency by estoppel occurs where one party 'holds out' to another that a person is acting as their agent.

Syllabus area D1(b)

12.4   C   Express authority is the authority actually granted by the principal to the agent. Ostensible authority is the authority that the agent represents to others that the agent has. What is usual or customary in the circumstances is implied authority.

Syllabus area D1(c)

12.5   A   The combination of express and implied authority is known as an agent's actual authority.

Syllabus area D1(c)

12.6   A   Unless circumstances indicate otherwise, the principal and third party will be liable under a contract formed by an agency relationship.

Syllabus area D1(d)

12.7   C   Only the principal and third party have rights and obligations under a contract formed under an agency relationship. Direct contact between them is not required to form a binding contract, the agent acts as a 'middle man' between them.

Syllabus area D1(d)

12.8   B   Accountancy practices are run as partnerships by partners.

Syllabus area D1(a)

12.9   C   The principal must have existed and had legal capacity when the contract was formed. The entire contract must be ratified. The principal must communicate their ratification clearly to the third party.

Syllabus area D1(b)

12.10   B   Agency by estoppel and implied agreement are known as agency without consent. A principal expressly consents to agency by express agreement and ratification.

Syllabus area D1(b)

12.11   D   Agency by necessity involves one party taking over another's goods in an emergency situation.

Syllabus area D1(b)

12.12   C   Ostensible authority includes whatever is usual in the circumstances plus whatever the principal impliedly gives the agent.

Syllabus area D1(c)

12.13   D   An agent's apparent authority is determined by what the principal has represented to others. A principal telling the agent their authority is express authority. What a third party determines the authority to be based on what is usual in the circumstances is implied usual authority.

Syllabus area D1(c)

12.14   D   The death, insanity or bankruptcy of a principal or agent will terminate the agency relationship. Otherwise agency will continue until the parties agree to terminate the relationship.

Syllabus area D1(c)

12.15   A   An agent will be liable on a contract if they intended to take personal liability, where it is usual business practice for them to be liable or where they act on their own behalf even though they purport to be acting for the principal.

Syllabus area D1(d)

13 Partnerships

13.1 C   A partner can be an individual person or a registered company. A partnership must just have the intention to be profitable and it can exist for a single business transaction.

Syllabus area D2(a)

13.2 B   In a limited partnership there is a partner who invests in the business but does not take part in the day-to-day running of the business.

Syllabus area D2(a)

13.3 B   To form an unlimited liability partnership the partners just need to decide to set up business together.

Syllabus area D2(b)

13.4 B   Partnership authority is based on agency law. Actual authority is determined by what the partners agree.

Syllabus area D2(c)

13.5 C   New partners are only liable for partnership debts that occur after they become a partner.

Syllabus area D2(c)

13.6 C   The bankruptcy of a partner will terminate the partnership.

Syllabus area D2(d)

13.7 A   When a partnership is terminated, external debts are paid off first.

Syllabus area D2(e)

13.8 C   An LLP must have two designated partners responsible for the publicity requirements of the partnership. A written partnership agreement is not required to form the partnership. The partnership does not dissolve when a partner leaves and is not exempt from audit.

Syllabus area D2(a)

13.9 A   An LLP is liable for its own debts. Partners are only liable for partnership debts up to the amount of their capital contribution. LLPs do have to file accounts with the Registrar of Companies and all partners may take part in the day-to-day running of the partnership.

Syllabus area D2(a)

13.10 B   Written partnership agreements are not required on formation of a partnership and, like any contract, may be created at any point. Terms in a written partnership agreement override terms in the Partnership Act 1890. They are not required by law when there are 20 partners and do not have to be in the form of a deed.

Syllabus area D2(b)

13.11 A   Partnerships can only grant fixed charges.

Syllabus area D2(d)

13.12 C   Retiring partners are liable for existing partnership debts, and those incurred after their retirement, unless third parties are notified of their retirement. This is because as far as third parties are aware, a partner is a partner until they are told they are no longer so.

Syllabus area D2(d)

13.13 A   To dissolve an LLP, it needs to be wound-up, in a similar way to a company.

Syllabus area D2(e)

13.14 A   Any surplus profit after all the other debts are repaid are distributed to the partners in the profit sharing ratio.

Syllabus area D2(e)

13.15 A   Under the Partnership Act 1890, notice by a partner and the end of an agreed fixed period of time for the partnership will result in its termination.

Syllabus area D2(e)

14 Corporations and legal personality

14.1 A   A benefit of running a business as a sole trader is that there are no formal procedures involved in setting one up. High dependence on the owner and an absence of economies of scale are disadvantages of being a sole trader.

Syllabus area D3(a)

14.2 B   All profits of a sole trader accrue to the owner. The business is not legally distinct from the owner and sole traders may need to register for VAT.

Syllabus area D3(a)

14.3 B   In a company limited by shares, a member's liability is limited to the amount of company share capital they have purchased, including any amounts outstanding.

Syllabus area D3(b)

14.4 C   Companies limited by guarantee do not have share capital.

Syllabus area D3(c)

14.5 C   The minimum issued share capital of a public company is £50,000.

Syllabus area D3(c)

14.6 B   Separate legal personality means that the company is responsible for its own debts. Members and directors are not protected from the force of the law because the veil of incorporation can be lifted. Members are liable up to the amount they have contributed in share capital if the company is insolvent.

Syllabus area D3(d)

14.7 A   Out of all the options, the courts will only lift the veil of incorporation with regard to fraudulent trading by a director.

Syllabus area D3(e)

14.8 C   A sole trader business is run by a single person who is not legally distinct from the business. The other options may be true for a sole trader, but they may also be true for various types of company and partnership as well.

Syllabus area D3(a)

14.9 B   Out of the options, a company limited by shares is the only one available to the group that will limit their liability to an amount that they agree to when the company is formed. On formation, each member will agree to a limit on their liability – the nominal value of their shares.

Syllabus area D3(b)

14.10 B   A public company is required to have a minimum of one member and two directors. Public companies cannot have unlimited liability. Public company names must end with 'plc'.

Syllabus area D3(c)

14.11 B   Net profit is not a criteria that must be met when qualifying for the small companies' regime. The other options are valid criteria.

Syllabus area D3(c)

14.12 A   A public company does not have to have its shares traded on a public stock exchange. If it does so, then it becomes known as a listed (or quoted) company.

Syllabus area D3(c)

14.13 C   Holding debentures in a company does not make that company a subsidiary. The other options are correct statements in regards to parent companies.

Syllabus area D3(c)

14.14 D   Separate legal personality can be ignored in certain circumstances (this is known as lifting the veil of incorporation).

Syllabus area D3(d)

14.15 A   The veil may be lifted to allow directors of insolvent companies to be found liable for their debts or to identify a group as a single economic entity. Lifting of the veil is not required in the other two options.

Syllabus area D3(e)

15 Company formation

15.1   A   The general duty of a promoter is reasonable skill and care.

Syllabus area D4(a)

15.2   B   Legally, pre-incorporation contracts cannot be ratified by the company.

Syllabus area D4(b)

15.3   A   The promoter and third party are liable on a pre-incorporation contract. The company never is.

Syllabus area D4(b)

15.4   A   Before it can trade, a public company must be issued with a trading certificate from the Registrar of Companies. None of the other options are criteria for obtaining a trading certificate.

Syllabus area D4(c)

15.5   B   A private company can trade as soon has it has obtained a certificate of incorporation from the Registrar of Companies. No trading certificate is required.

Syllabus area D4(c)

15.6   B   Keeping a register of debentureholders is not a legal requirement, although most companies will hold such a register. The other options are company books that a public company is required by law to keep.

Syllabus area D4(d)

15.7   C   A register of directors must include a service address for each director. It does not include a list of shadow directors. It should be available for members to inspect for free.

Syllabus area D4(d)

15.8   D   The role of a promoter is to form a company.

Syllabus area D4(a)

15.9   C   Where a promoter acts as an agent for others, they must not put themselves into a position where their own interests clash with those of the company. Accountants acting in a professional capacity are not promoters. A promoter may make a legitimate profit as a result of their position. There is nothing to stop a promoter from owning shares in the company that they form.

Syllabus area D4(a)

15.10 D   Buying an 'off-the-shelf' company and novating the contract are two ways that a promoter can avoid liability on a pre-incorporation contract. The other options will not prevent the promoter from being liable.

Syllabus area D4(b)

15.11 A   All the documents, except for the articles of association, must be sent to the Registrar to register a company. If articles of association are not submitted then the company will be issued with model articles relevant to the type of company being formed.

Syllabus area D4(c)

15.12 C   The date on the certificate of incorporation is conclusive proof of the date of incorporation.

Syllabus area D4(c)

15.13 D   A public company must re-register as a public company if its share capital falls below £50,000.

Syllabus area D4(c)

15.14 C   The Registrar is responsible for registering all companies and for issuing Certificates of Incorporation. They also file copies of special resolutions sent in by each company. The Register of Members is only held by the company itself.

Syllabus area D4(d)

15.15 A   Private companies must keep their accounting records for three years, public companies for six years.

Syllabus area D4(d)

16 Constitution of a company

16.1   C   It is the subscribers who sign the memorandum of association.

Syllabus area D4(e)

16.2   A   Model articles of association describe how the company is to be managed and administered. Companies can use any version of model articles that they like and members are free to amend their contents.

Syllabus area D4(f)

16.3   C   Model articles of association may refer to the objects of the company, but this is not the same as the mission statement. The other options are examples taken from the content of model articles.

Syllabus area D4(f)

16.4   B   A special or written resolution with a 75% majority is sufficient to change a company's articles. There is no restriction on the number of times per year the articles may be changed. Copies of the amended articles must be submitted to the Registrar with 15 days of the amendment taking effect.

Syllabus area D4(g)

16.5   C   Changes to company articles that conflict with the Companies Act are void. The other options are valid changes.

Syllabus area D4(g)

16.6   A   A company may be required to change its name if it is deemed offensive. It may set its own rules for changing its name, and names that suggest a connection with the Government are permitted providing the appropriate permission is granted.

Syllabus area D4(h)

16.7   A   A company may change its name but not its domicile.

Syllabus area D4(h)

16.8 A   A company's constitution contractually binds the company and members in their capacity as members.

Syllabus area D4(e)

16.9 C   S40 of the Companies Act 2006 protects the interests of third parties when a contract with a company is outside the scope of the company's objects.

Syllabus area D4(e)

16.10 B   Payment of dividends and appointment of directors are included in the content of model articles of association. Payment of charitable donations and formation of a remuneration committee are not included.

Syllabus area D4(f)

16.11 D   Communication with members is covered by model articles of association. Model articles differ depending on the type of company. They do not contain clauses on remuneration of employees or ethical treatment of suppliers.

Syllabus area D4(f)

16.12 C   A change to a company's articles is permitted providing it does not conflict with the Companies Act 2006 or general law. A company may set its own procedure for changing its name but may not perform an illegal act. Changes that compel a member to subscribe for additional shares or increase their liability on the shares they own are not permitted.

Syllabus area D4(g)

16.13 A   Any change must be for the benefit of the company as a whole (including the forced transfer of shares from the minority to the majority). A minority can prevent a change that unjustly discriminates against them. A majority may make a change that the minority feels is prejudicial to their interests.

Syllabus area D4(g)

16.14 A   No name may be offensive or sensitive as defined by the Secretary of State. Some private companies may omit 'Ltd' from their name. Names that suggest a connection with government are not void but official approval is required to use them. Welsh companies are not required to end their name with '(Cym)'.

Syllabus area D4(h)

16.15 D   An injunction can prevent the use of a properly registered company name. A court may refuse an injunction if the businesses are sufficiently different in nature because the chance of customer confusion is low. Courts and the Company Names Adjudicators may change a company's name if necessary. Failure to refer to the Company Names Adjudicators first will not stop a passing-off action from succeeding.

Syllabus area D4(h)

17 MTQ Bank 3

17.1

Text reference. Chapter 11.

Top tips. You need to consider the authority of partners and the liability they have for the firm's debts. Avoid the temptation to discuss all you know about agency law – keep your answer focused on partnerships.

(a) Sam has taken money from the firm's bank account to use for a personal holiday. However, as a partner, and in the absence of any specific mention to the contrary in the agreement, he has authority to withdraw money from the bank account. His action has therefore incurred a debt to a third party that is owed by all three partners, not just himself, and if he cannot repay the money to the bank, the bank is entitled to sue the other partners for the balance.

(b) Tam entered into a contract to buy bicycles in the name of the partnership. The partnership agreement specifies that the partnership should only sell petrol, so Tam does not have authority to undertake this contract. However, the third party is not privy to the partnership agreement so is not aware that the contract is beyond the scope of the partnership. Tam has apparent authority to undertake the contract on behalf of the other partners who are liable on the contract.

(c) Purchasing petrol is a normal part of business for this partnership. Whoever made the contract would have had authority to do so and bound the other partners to the contract. They are all liable for the petrol bill.

17.2

Text reference. Chapters 12 and 13.

Top tips. This is a straightforward question. Keep your answer brief but cover all necessary points. Avoid going into detail about the *Salomon* case.

(a) Separate corporate personality means that company is distinct as a separate legal person from its owners or members and hence a 'veil of incorporation' exists between them. The distinction between a company and its members was clearly set out in *Salomon v Salomon & Co Ltd 1897*.

(b) A consequence of registering his business as a company is separate legal personality and limited liability. The benefits to Mick are:

Mick's company can enter into the new contracts in its own right and only it (rather than Mick) will be liable for damages for any breach of contract.

The company will be liable for its own debts should repayment become a problem.

The company, rather than Mick, will be liable of any negligence claims made against the business.

The limit of Mick's liability in respect of the business will be any amount unpaid on his shares. This likely to be substantially less than the current situation where Mick is liable in full for all liabilities of the business.

17.3

Text reference. Chapter 12.

Top tips. This question also highlights the importance of reading the major cases in the Study Text. If you had then you would recognise the two situations and have a fast track to the correct answer.

(a) The first consequence of limited liability is that a company itself is liable without limit for its own debts. If the company buys goods from a supplier it owes the supplier money. Limited liability is a benefit to members. They own the business, so might be the people whom the creditors logically ask to pay the debts of the company if the company is unable to pay them itself. Limited liability prevents this by stipulating the creditors of a limited company cannot demand payment of the company's debts from members of the company (*MacDonald v Costello 2011*).

(b) In the case of his contract with Ed Ltd, Doc cannot pursue Ed Ltd's debt by suing Ed. This is because Ed is only a member of Ed Ltd and has no liability for the company's debts (*Salomon v Salomon & Co Ltd 1897*). This point was more recently reinforced in the case of *MacDonald v Costello*. However, Doc may be able to pursue a claim on the basis that Ed, as shareholder and sole director of Ed Ltd, knew that the company was insolvent when it entered into the contract with Doc and therefore was trading fraudulently. If he is successful then the veil of incorporation may be lifted by the Insolvency Act and he may seek payment from Ed himself.

(c)   Fitt has a legal obligation not to pursue Doc's clients and by setting up Gen Ltd he has attempted to use the veil of corporate personality to evade this obligation. The case of *Gilford Motor Co Ltd v Horne 1933* suggests that the court would find in favour of Doc and enforce the agreement between Doc and Fitt.

17.4

> **Text reference**. Chapter 13.
>
> **Top tips**. Make sure that you address all three of the issues and get the easy marks by stating what the law says in each case.

(a)   The general rule is that a promoter is personally liable on any completed pre-incorporation contract entered into with a third party. A pre-incorporation contract is a contract purported to be made by a company or its agent at a time before the company has received its certificate of incorporation.

In the situation involving the computer equipment, the directors of Eden plc are not legally bound to honour the purported contract with the supplier. The supplier will have to take action against Don for breach of contract.

(b)   In the situation described involving the patent, there is no contract involving the company because the company did not exist when the contract was formed. If the other party does not wish to proceed with the agreement, the directors of Eden plc will be unable to show any obligation for them to do so.

(c)   In the situation described involving the business equipment, there is no contract since Eden plc does not wish to pursue the arrangements with Fad Ltd. Fad Ltd therefore has no cause of action against either Don or the company. This is because the 'contract' was 'subject to adoption by Eden plc' and this condition never happened - therefore the contract is not valid.

17.5

> **Text reference**. Chapter 14.
>
> **Top tips**. Remember the rules concerning how a company may change its articles. It may come up regularly in this exam.

(a)   The Companies Act 2006 provides that a company's articles of association bind a company to its members, the members to the company and members to members. Members are deemed to have separately covenanted with each other and the company to observe the provisions of the articles.

(b)   A company's articles of association may be altered by passing a special resolution to that effect in general meeting. As a private company, Glad Ltd may also pass an written resolution to the same effect with a 75% majority.

(c)   A change to a company's articles is generally valid if it is of benefit to the company, and this certainly appears to apply in Fred's case (he is in direct competition with Glad Ltd). However, in *Dafen Tinplate Co Ltd v Llanelly Steel Co (1907) Ltd 1920* a similar amendment was held to be invalid because it permitted the company to acquire the shares of any member, even if there were no specific grounds to show that it would benefit the company. The resolution actually proposed by Glad Ltd is the same because it would allow the company to acquire the shares of any member for a fair price. Therefore it is likely to be held as invalid under the facts of the *Dafen* case.

18 Share capital

18.1   A   A public company must have a minimum of one member.

Syllabus area E1(a)

18.2   C   Ordinary shares may or may not have voting rights attached. Dividends do not have to be paid every year and ordinary shares do not entitle the shareholder to have their capital repaid ahead of other creditors on liquidation.

Syllabus area E1(b)

18.3   C   Any limited company may create treasury shares by purchasing its own shares for cash or out of distributable profit. It cannot exercise voting rights attaching to the shares, but may re-issue them for cash without the usual issuing formalities.

Syllabus area E1(b)

18.4   B   A public offer is where the public subscribe for shares directly to the company. An offer for sale is an offer to the public to buy shares based on information in a prospectus. A placing involves individuals or institutions being offered shares in a small number of large blocks based on agreement to buy shares at a pre-determined price.

Syllabus area E1(c)

18.5   A   A rights issue is an offer to existing shareholders to buy further shares in the company. A bonus issue is the allotment of additional shares to shareholders in proportion to their holdings.

Syllabus area E1(c)

18.6   C   Shares may be issued at a premium to their nominal value and the premium is credited to the share premium account. Therefore shares do not have to be issued at their nominal value. Shares must not be issued at a discount to their nominal value.

Syllabus area E1(d)

18.7   C   The company does not have to receive the full nominal value of the share when it is issued. Such shares are known as partly-paid shares. Any balance owing transfers to the new shareholder if the share is sold.

Syllabus area E1(d)

18.8   A   Called-up share capital is the amount the company has required shareholders to pay on existing shares. A company's issued share capital is the type, class, number and amount of shares issued to shareholders. The amount existing shareholders have paid on existing shares is the paid-up share capital.

Syllabus area E1(a)

18.9   D   A share's market value is based on the prospects of the company and may be equal, greater or lower than nominal value.

Syllabus area E1(a)

18.10   B   Preference shareholders do not usually have the right to vote in company meetings but they do have the right to have their capital repaid ahead of ordinary shareholders in the event of a liquidation. On liquidation, preference shareholders usually have no right to share in any surplus assets. A company is not compelled to pay a dividend on preference shares.

Syllabus area E1(b)

18.11   D   Class rights are rights that attach to a specific class of share. It would therefore be a variation of class rights if the amount of dividend payable on a class of preference share is changed. The other options are examples of what does not constitute a variation of class rights.

Syllabus area E1(b)

18.12   A   Only directors of private companies with one class of share have the power to allot shares unless restricted by the articles. Directors of all other companies must have authority from the members to do so.

Syllabus area E1(c)

18.13   A   Pre-emption rights only apply when a company proposes to allot ordinary shares wholly for cash.

Syllabus area E1(c)

18.14   C   A private company may accept goods or services for payment at an over-value. No independent valuation is required. A public company may issue shares for non-cash consideration and at least 25% of the nominal value of the shares must be paid up on allotment.

Syllabus area E1(d)

18.15 A   The permitted uses of a share premium account are to issue fully paid shares under a bonus issue or pay issue expenses and commissions in respect of a new share issue.

Syllabus area E1(d)

19 Loan capital

19.1 A   All companies registered under the Companies Act 2006 have an implied power to borrow.

Syllabus area E2(a)

19.2 A   Pari passu means that all debentures rank equally.

Syllabus area E2(b)

19.3 B   Interest on debentures must be paid and is tax-deductible. Dividends are only paid if the directors declare them and payment is not tax-deductible. In the event of liquidation, debentureholders have their investment repaid before anything is returned to the shareholders.

Syllabus area E2(c)

19.4 B   A fixed charge will always have priority over a floating charge created before it if the fixed chargeholder was not aware of the other charge.

Syllabus area E2(d)

19.5 B   Active intervention by the chargee, such as appointing a receiver will cause the charge to crystallise. The other options will not cause the charge to crystallise.

Syllabus area E2(d)

19.6 C   Charges must be registered within 21 days of creation.

Syllabus area E2(e)

19.7 C   A charge may be registered late but only if it does not prejudice the creditors or shareholders of the company.

Syllabus area E2(e)

19.8 C   A loan contract that is beyond the powers of the directors may be ratified by the company if it is within the capacity of the company. Charges are not required for a loan contract to be enforceable. Loan contracts are enforceable by the lender even if they are ultra vires.

Syllabus area E2(a)

19.9 B   Out of the options, only debenture stock must be created using a debenture trust deed. Single and series debentures may use a debenture trust deed but this is not compulsory.

Syllabus area E2(b)

19.10 A   A debenture trust deed creates security for the debentures via charges. A single person (a trustee) is appointed. This means the company only has to deal with one person rather than a number of individual debentureholders. Debentures covered by a debenture trust deed do not have a higher priority of repayment and are not necessarily faster to sell.

Syllabus area E2(b)

19.11 A   Share capital does not have to be repaid, unlike a loan which must be repaid at some point. Share capital has voting rights but loan capital does not. Loan capital offers the holder more security than share capital because it has a higher priority to be repaid and may be secured on assets by a charge. Both loan and share capital are transferrable.

Syllabus area E2(c)

19.12 C   The public sale of shares and debentures are both known as a prospectus. The other options are true statements.

Syllabus area E2(c)

19.13 A   A 'negative pledge' clause prevents the company from issuing subsequent charges on the same asset.

Syllabus area E2(d)

19.14 C   Negative pledge clauses are used by floating chargeholders to prevent subsequent fixed charges being secured on the same asset.

Syllabus area E2(d)

19.15 A   A charge must be registered within 21 days of creation or the company and officers that created it will be liable for a fine. A court order is required to rectify a mistake in the registration documents. The Registrar cannot deem non-registered charges as valid and enforceable.

Syllabus area E2(e)

20 Capital maintenance and dividend law

20.1 A   The principle of capital maintenance states that companies should not make payments out of their capital to the detriment of creditors.

Syllabus area E3(a)

20.2 C   There are no restrictions on a limited company concerning the cancellation of unissued shares because such a change will not affect its financial position.

Syllabus area E3(a)

20.3 B   A private company may reduce its share capital without application to a court if it passes a special resolution and obtains a statement of solvency from the directors.

Syllabus area E3(a)

20.4 B   A special resolution and court approval are required for a public company to reduce its share capital.

Syllabus area E3(a)

20.5 A   Scrip dividends are paid by issuing additional shares.

Syllabus area E3(b)

20.6 A   A dividend becomes a debt of the company when it is declared.

Syllabus area E3(b)

20.7 C   A capital redemption reserve is an undistributable reserve. Dividends may be paid out of retained earnings or accumulated realised profits.

Syllabus area E3(b)

20.8 B   The rules on capital maintenance exist to protect the interest of a company's creditors.

Syllabus area E3(a)

20.9 C   Buying back shares using cash not surplus profit is not a method of reducing share capital permitted by the Companies Act. The other options are valid methods of reducing share capital.

Syllabus area E3(a)

20.10 B   A solvency statement must be made 15 days before the meeting where the special resolution to reduce the company's share capital will be voted on. It is an offence to make a solvency statement without reasonable grounds. All the company's directors must be named on the statement and solvency statements must declare that the company should be able to pay its debts for the next 12 months.

Syllabus area E3(a)

20.11 B   Public companies must have a minimum share capital of £50,000. If any reduction takes the value to below £50,000 then the company must re-register as a private company.

Syllabus area E3(a)

20.12 C   Dividends paid part of the way through a company's financial year are known as interim dividends. Dividends paid in specie are paid using a method other than cash.

Syllabus area E3(b)

20.13 C   Depreciation in the current year is a realised loss that is included in the calculation of distributable profit. Asset revaluations are unrealised and not included. Only realised profits in the current or previous financial years are included. A premium received on issuing shares goes to the share premium account and is not included in the profits available for distribution.

Syllabus area E3(b)

20.14 D   A public company may make a distribution as long as its net assets are not less than its share capital plus its undistributable reserves

Syllabus area E3(b)

20.15 A   Directors who know dividends are unlawful will be liable, but those who honestly rely on proper accounts when making the decision to pay the dividend are not liable. Liability is in civil law not criminal law. Members who did not know the payment was unlawful are not liable.

Syllabus area E3(b)

21 MTQ Bank 4

21.1

> **Text reference**. Chapter 15.
>
> **Top tips**. This type of question simply requires you to apply your knowledge to some simple facts. You must, however, know the meaning of the terms before you can answer it!

(a)   A company's issued share capital is the type, class, number and amount of shares actually held by its shareholders. Therefore it is the term related to the number of shares held by shareholders.

(b)   Paid-up share capital is the amount of a company's issued share capital that it has actually received payment for from the shareholders. It is therefore the term related to the amount of money received by the company from shareholders for their shares.

(c)   The Companies Act states that for a public limited company, the issued share capital must be at least £50,000 of which at least one quarter plus the full amount of any share premium must be paid up.

21.2

> **Text reference**. Chapters 15 and 17.
>
> **Top tips**. Once you have stated the general rule on issuing shares at a discount, it is simple to apply it to the facts in the scenario.

(a)   There is a general rule on issuing shares that states shares with a nominal value may be issued at a premium to that value but may not be issued at a discount to it: s580 and *Ooregum Gold Mining Co of India v Roper 1892.*

(b)   Under the Companies Act, Flop Ltd had a remaining call on Gus after the first issue for the amount left unpaid on his shares of (10,000 × 25p = £2,500). This is because, when a company issues shares at a discount to their nominal value it is effectively saying that the shareholder has a £1 share, say, but only needs to pay 75p in total for it. This is prohibited: the shareholder must nonetheless pay the full nominal value plus interest at the appropriate rate.

(c)   The same rule also applies to the second issue to Gus. Flop Ltd is trying to issue shares at a 50p discount to their nominal value. This is disallowed under the Companies Act and Gus is liable for the balance (10,000 × 50p = £5,000) plus interest.

21.3

(a)   A company's shares confer certain rights on the members who own them. Where only one type of share exists the rights are normally the same, however different types of share will often confer different rights. For example preference shares usually entitle the member to a fixed dividend with priority of payment over ordinary shares and priority over the repayment of capital (ahead of ordinary shares) in the event of a winding up. Other class rights may attach regarding voting or the right to remove a director. Any share that has different rights from others is grouped with the other shares carrying identical rights to form a class.

(b)   Class rights may be varied providing a special resolution is passed by members of that class. For an alteration to be valid the majority must honestly believe that it is in the interest of the company as a whole and that it would be in the interests of a hypothetical individual member: *Greenhalgh v Arderne Cinemas Ltd 1950*. A minority of members that hold at least 15% of the shares of the class may apply to the court to have a variation cancelled.

The reduction of dividends proposed by the directors of Lux Ltd is clearly a variation of a class right that under the statutory variation procedure requires a 75% majority by special or written resolution. Kudos Ltd is likely to want to prevent this variation but as it only holds 20% of the shares in the class it cannot prevent the variation by itself. However, Kudos Ltd does hold over 15% of the shares in the class so it could apply to the court for the variation to be cancelled. As the effect on Kudos Ltd is relatively minor and as it affects all shareholders equally it is likely that the court would uphold the variation.

21.4

(a)   A company is not required to keep a register of debentureholders unless debentures are issued as a series or as debenture stock. Neither applies in Milly Ltd's case and therefore no register of debentureholders is required.

(b)   Although the charge documentation states that a fixed charge was created, Milly Ltd may deal with the charged asset as it wishes to. This fulfils the criteria for a floating charge and therefore the charge will be registered as a floating charge.

(c)   Peppa Ltd's charge, whilst created first, was not registered within 21 days. It is therefore not valid. Otto Ltd's charge was validly registered and therefore will take priority in the event of liquidation.

21.5

(a)   Only accumulated profit is a distributable reserve out of which dividend's may be paid. In Fan Ltd's case the total is £3,000 for the year and no profits were brought forward from previous years. The profit on revaluation of land and buildings is credited to the revaluation reserve, not to the profit and loss reserve and is not distributable.

For the year in question, £4,000 was paid as a dividend. The payment would only be legal if the company had accumulated realised profits equal to or greater than £4,000. The company only had £3,000 and therefore the payment is illegal.

(b)   Dee and Eff will be liable as directors (for declaring unlawful dividends) and as shareholders (who knew or had reasonable grounds to believe the dividend was unlawful) because the dividend paid was in excess of the company's distributable profit.

22 Company directors

22.1   A   A de jure director is expressly appointed. A de facto director is held out by the company to be a director. A shadow director is neither, they are a person whose instructions the actual directors are accustomed to follow.

Syllabus area F1(a)

22.2   A   Company directors must be at least 16 years old.

Syllabus area F1(b)

22.3   C   At the first AGM of a public company, all the directors are required to retire.

Syllabus area F1(b)

22.4   A   A CEO's actual authority is whatever the board gives to them.

Syllabus area F1(c)

22.5   A   The power of a company's directors is defined in its Articles of Association.

Syllabus area F1(c)

22.6   B   A director owes their statutory duties to the company as a whole.

Syllabus area F1(d)

22.7   A   Directors will be liable for a company's debts if the Articles of Association say that they are. There may be financial penalties for a director who breaches their fiduciary duties, but taking over personal responsibility for the company's debts is unlikely to be one of them.

Syllabus area F1(d)

22.8   B   A de jure director is expressly appointed. A de facto director is held out by the company to be a director. A shadow director is neither, they are a person whose instructions the actual directors are accustomed to follow. An alternate director is appointed by a director of a company to attend and vote for them at board meetings they are unable to attend.

Syllabus area F1(a)

22.9   B   Non-executive directors are not involved in the day-to-day running of the company. A de facto director is held out by the company to be a director. A shadow director is a person whose instructions the actual directors are accustomed to follow. All directors are subject to statutory duties.

Syllabus area F1(a)

22.10 C   Being a director of an insolvent company or being unfit to be concerned in the management of a company are the two grounds where a court must disqualify. The other options are grounds where they court may disqualify.

Syllabus area F1(b)

22.11 B   The removal of a company director from office requires an ordinary resolution with special notice.

Syllabus area F1(b)

22.12 C   Directors should use their powers for a proper purpose that they honestly believe to be in the best interests of the company.

Syllabus area F1(c)

22.13 B   Members can ratify such actions but an ordinary resolution is required.

Syllabus area F1(c)

22.14 D   Directors who consider the long-term consequences of their decisions on employees are meeting their duty to promote the success of the company.

Syllabus area F1(d)

expected of a person who is carrying out their function and the levels that they actually have.

Syllabus area F1(d)

22.15 A   A director is expected to show the level of knowledge, skill and experience that is reasonably expected of a person who is carrying out their function and the levels that they actually have.

Syllabus area F1(d)

23 Other company officers

23.1   C   Only a public limited company must have a company secretary.

Syllabus area F2(a)

23.2   A   A company's sole director may not act as company secretary. A company's accountant or solicitor may act as company secretary.

Syllabus area F2(a)

23.3   B   A company secretary is appointed by the directors.

Syllabus area F2(a)

23.4   C   Accountancy firms often audit the accounts that they have prepared. Employees of a company and their partners are expressly prevented from acting as company auditor.

Syllabus area F2(b)

23.5   C   The directors appoint the first ever auditors of their company.

Syllabus area F2(b)

23.6   B   Only auditors of private companies are deemed automatically reappointed unless specific circumstances apply.

Syllabus area F2(b)

23.7   B   The statutory duty of an auditor is to report to the members on the truth and fairness of the accounts and whether the accounts have been prepared in accordance with the Companies Act.

Syllabus area F2(b)

23.8   D   It is the Board of Directors that sets the specific duties of the company secretary.

Syllabus area F2(a)

23.9   C   A company secretary has the power to bind the company in contracts related to the administrative side of the company only. It was decided in *Panorama Developments (Guildford) Ltd v Fidelis Furnishing Fabrics Ltd 1971* that this includes a contract for hiring cars to transport customers.

Syllabus area F2(a)

23.10 A   A company secretary would expect to be responsible for establishing and maintaining the company's statutory registers and filing accurate company returns with the Registrar of Companies.

Syllabus area F2(a)

23.11 C   A full member of the ACCA is qualified to act as a company secretary. Employment as a plc's company secretary is also valid qualification, but the employment must be for three out of the five preceding years.

Syllabus area F2(a)

23.12 C   A company auditor has the right, at all times, to access the books, accounts and vouchers of the company.

Syllabus area F2(b)

23.13 B   As with directors, an ordinary resolution with special notice is required to remove an auditor from office.

Syllabus area F2(b)

23.14 C   Where an auditor of a non-quoted company is removed at a general meeting they must provide members and creditors with a statement of whether there is anything that should be brought to their attention.

Syllabus area F2(b)

23.15 A   A private company is exempt from audit if its turnover is less than £6.5 million, its balance sheet total is less than £3.26 million and it has fewer than 50 employees on average.

Syllabus area F2(b)

24 Company meetings and resolutions

24.1 A   Only public limited companies must hold annual general meetings.

Syllabus area F3(a)

24.2 B   21 days' notice must be given in respect of annual general meetings.

Syllabus area F3(a)

24.3 A   14 days' notice is required for a special resolution.

Syllabus area F3(b)

24.4 B   An ordinary resolution requires a simple majority of the votes cast to be passed. 50% is not enough because no majority is achieved and those voting against the resolution can have the same number of votes. 51% is therefore the minimum.

Syllabus area F3(b)

24.5 C   90% of the members of a private company may agree to a shorter notice period.

Syllabus area F3(c)

24.6 A   Members controlling 5% of the voting rights may requisition a resolution at an annual general meeting.

Syllabus area F3(c)

24.7 A   On a vote on a show of hands, each member receives one vote.

Syllabus area F3(c)

24.8 C   Approving dividends is included in the ordinary business of an AGM.

Syllabus area F3(a)

24.9 D   The alteration of the Articles requires a special resolution. The other items of business require an ordinary resolution.

Syllabus area F3(a)

24.10 B   The text of special resolutions must be included in the meeting notice and copies must be sent to the Registrar for filing. Both types of resolution require 14 days' notice and both can be voted on via a show of hands or a poll.

Syllabus area F3(b)

24.11 A   Only private companies may pass written resolutions.

Syllabus area F3(b)

24.12 A   Removal of an auditor (or a director) are the only items of business that may not be achieved by a written resolution.

Syllabus area F3(b)

24.13 B   Special notice is 28 days.

Syllabus area F3(c)

24.14 D   Members must make their request and identify the resolution six weeks before the meeting.

Syllabus area F3(c)

24.15 C   Proxies may speak at a meeting and demand a poll. They may vote on a show of hands and a poll. They may not requisition a meeting.

Syllabus area F3(c)

25 MTQ Bank 5

25.1

> **Text reference**. Chapter 18.
>
> **Top tips**. To answer part (b) well you need to have learned and understood the statutory duties of a director. Applying them in this case is relatively straightforward.

(a)   Since they make contracts as agents of the company and have control of its property, directors are said to be akin to trustees and therefore owe fiduciary duties to the company. A fiduciary duty is one based on common law principles of trust and honesty. Therefore a director must act bona fide and honestly and not seek any personal advantage when dealing with the company.

(b)   Turning to the case in question, it appears that Caz has not disclosed either her interest in Era Ltd or her interest in this particular contract. Under s177 of the Companies Act, the interest should have been stated at the board meeting that Caz attended that approved the contract. It was not. It should also have been declared under s182 of the Companies Act once it had occurred – but it was not either. She will therefore have to account to Dull plc for any profit that she makes on the transaction and she may also be subject to a fine. Had she dealt honestly with Dull plc by declaring her interest and obtaining company approval, she would have been permitted to retain any profit that is made.

25.2

> **Text reference**. Chapter 18.
>
> **Top tips**. Don't forget that it is the perspective of the third party that is important when determining whether a company is liable for contracts entered into by one of its agents.

(a)   A director's express authority to enter into a particular contract is granted formally by the board of directors. Where such express authority is given, the company will be bound by the agreement.

(b)   Where there is no express authority, authority may be implied from the director's position within the company. Chief Executive Officers usually have authority to make commercial contracts on behalf of the company and therefore those appointed as such are permitted to exercise this authority as they see fit, their actions binding the company.

(c)   The circumstances in which Katch Ltd finds itself are very similar to that of the *Freeman & Lockyer v Buckhurst Park Properties (Mangal) Ltd 1964* case. Len has been allowed by the board to act as if he were Chief Execute Officer and therefore as a third party Mo is entitled to assume that he has the implied authority of one. This authority permits him to bind the company in commercial contracts, so the company will be bound by the advertising contract entered into by Len. Katch Ltd therefore has a liability to pay Mo or be sued for breach of contract.

25.3

> **Text reference**. Chapter 18.
>
> **Top tips**. You must learn the types of director to be able to attempt questions such as this.

(a)   Mills was appointed as a director on registration and is therefore a de jure director.

(b)   Beni was not officially appointed as a director but is held out to be the company's managing director on its paperwork. He runs the business on Boo's instructions and is therefore a de facto director.

(c)   Boo has not been appointed as a director, nor is she held out by the company to be a director. However, because the director (Mills) is accustomed to act on her instructions (via Beni) she is a shadow director of the company.

25.4

> **Text reference**. Chapter 19.
>
> **Top tips**. Not all questions require you to explain the facts of a case, but when you are required to explain an area of law it may be a very good idea to refer to cases in detail. However you would have also scored marks if you illustrated your answer with a hypothetical situation instead.
>
> **Easy marks**. Stating the private company rule in Part (a) and remembering the cases in Part (b). There are very few cases on company secretaries so you should try to remember them all.

(a)   Private limited companies are not required by law to have a company secretary. Therefore Envy Ltd does not need to have one.

(b)   The powers of the company secretary have historically been very limited, but the common law increasingly recognises that they may be able to act as agents in some circumstances. Specifically, they may enter the company into contracts connected with the administrative side of the company: *Panorama Developments (Guildford) Ltd v Fidelis Furnishing Fabrics Ltd 1971*. Envy Ltd will not be bound by the contract because it is commercial, rather than administrative, in nature.

(c)   Under the Companies Act, a sole director may not be appointed as company secretary. Therefore Vic will have to appoint someone else or decide that the company does not need a company secretary. This is permissible because as a limited company, Envy Ltd is not required to have a company secretary.

25.5

> **Text reference**. Chapters 19 and 20.
>
> **Top tips**. Part (c) shows how there can be some overlap between areas of the F4 syllabus. You must also be aware of the rules concerning calling and conducting a company meetings.

(a)   The ordinary business to be transacted at an annual general meeting includes the consideration of the directors' and auditors' reports and the company accounts, the election of directors and appointment of auditors, the fixing of auditors' remuneration and the declaration of dividends.

(b)   Every public company must hold an annual general meeting in each calendar year within six months of the company's year-end. At least 21 days' written notice must be given unless all members entitled to attend agree to shorter notice. Therefore, although the meeting was held in the correct time after the company's year-end, there was insufficient notice given because not all the shareholders agreed to the shorter notice.

(c)   Under the Companies Act, a general meeting can be called by an auditor who gives a statement detailing the circumstances for their resignation or other loss of office and requires their explanation to be considered by the company. Therefore the directors must uphold the request.

26 Insolvency and administration

26.1   B   The members always commence a voluntary winding-up.

Syllabus area G1(a)

26.2   A   Although a voluntary winding-up up is commenced by the members, it is the solvency of the company that determines whether it is a members' or creditors' voluntary winding-up. If the company is solvent then it is a members' voluntary winding-up, if it is insolvent then it is a creditors' voluntary winding-up.

Syllabus area G1(a)

26.3   B   Creditors owed more than £750 and who sent a written demand for payment but have not heard from the company in 21 days may request the compulsory winding-up of the company. The other parties may not request the compulsory winding-up of a company.

Syllabus area G1(b)

26.4   B   The just and equitable ground will be applied where the object of the company cannot be achieved. For example where the company only existed to 'work a particular patent' *Re German Date Coffee Co 1882*. The other options are not grounds for the just and equitable winding-up of a company.

Syllabus area G1(b)

26.5   C   When a company is liquidated, the members share any surplus remaining after all the other debts have been repaid.

Syllabus area G1(c)

26.6   C   The main purpose of administration is to attempt to rescue the company as a going concern. During this time the company will be protected from legal action but this is not the purpose of administration.

Syllabus area G1(d)

26.7   A   Only floating chargeholders, directors and the company itself may appoint an administrator without a court order.

Syllabus area G1(e)

26.8   C   A liquidator is in charge of a voluntary winding-up. The official receiver is in charge of a compulsory winding-up. An administrator is in charge of an administration.

Syllabus area G1(a)

26.9   A   A members' voluntary winding-up commences as soon as the necessary resolution is passed.

Syllabus area G1(a)

26.10 D   Only the members can commence a creditors' voluntary winding up. They can do so with either a special resolution or written resolution with a 75% majority (private companies only).

Syllabus area G1(a)

26.11 C   The official receiver is the liquidator in charge of a compulsory liquidation.

Syllabus area G1(b)

26.12 C   The order for a compulsory liquidation must be published in The Gazette.

Syllabus area G1(b)

26.13 A   The liquidator has the highest priority for payment when a company is liquidated.

Syllabus area G1(c)

26.14 D   If a company cannot be rescued as a going concern then the next objective of administration is to achieve a better result for creditors than an immediate winding-up. Liquidation and administration are

mutually exclusive, a winding-up order cannot be made if an administration order is already in place. Administrations may be made by certain parties without a court order. An administrator is put in charge of a company in administration.

Syllabus area G1(d)

26.15 A   A period of administration ends twelve months after it commenced or following the success of the administration. It may also end following a court order granted on application by the administrator or a creditor, or if an improper motive for applying for administration is discovered.

Syllabus area G1(e)

27 MTQ Bank 6

27.1

Text reference. Chapter 21.

Top tips. Don't forget that the company instigates a voluntary winding-up, it is whether the directors issue a statement of solvency that makes it a members' or creditors' voluntary winding-up. You must know the grounds for compulsory liquidation.

(a)   A voluntary winding-up is instigated by a company resolution that states that the company cannot continue to trade. For the winding-up to be a members' voluntary winding-up, the directors must issue a statement of solvency. If they do not issue a statement of solvency then the winding-up is a creditors' voluntary winding up.

(b)   A compulsory winding-up is one ordered by the court under s.122 Insolvency Act 1986 on one or more of seven specified grounds. One of these grounds is that it is just and equitable to wind-up the company.

A member who is dissatisfied with the directors or controlling shareholders over the management of the company may petition the court for a winding-up on the basis that to do so is just and equitable. Such winding-up orders have been made where there is a complete deadlock in the management of the company's affairs *(Re Yenidje Tobacco Co Ltd 1916)* and where the trust and confidence between both directors and shareholders in a small company have broken down *(Ebrahimi v Westbourne Galleries Ltd 1973)*.

Due to the complete deadlock in the management of the company's affairs, and the lack of trust between the brothers, it is likely that a court will order it to be wound-up on the just and equitable ground.

27.2

Text reference. Chapter 21.

Top tips. Note that the question relates to compulsory winding-up; do not get side tracked into other types of liquidation.

(a)   Under s122 Insolvency Act 1986, where a creditor is owed more than £750 and makes a written demand for payment and the company fails to pay the debt, or offer reasonable security for it, within three weeks, the company is deemed unable to pay its debts. Therefore Aero Ltd may seek the compulsory winding up of Getz Ltd.

(b)   The effect of the compulsory liquidation on the areas identified by Aspin are:

The company may not dispose of the office building from the commencement of the liquidation unless approved by the court.

The creditor may not commence legal action against the company except with the leave of the court.

The employment of the company's staff ceases unless the liquidator retains them to carry on the business.

The company's floating charges will crystallise. The creditors will be paid in accordance with the priority of charges and funds available from the assets.

27.3

> **Text reference**. Chapter 21.
>
> **Top tips**. At all times remember the purpose of administration. It is not a winding up, but an attempt to save the business. Do not stray off the subject matter or you will lose marks and waste time.

(a) An administration order is an order of the court that puts an insolvency practitioner in control of the company with a defined programme for rescuing the company from insolvency as a going concern. Its effect is to insulate the company from its creditors while it seeks, to save itself, or failing that, to achieve a better result for creditors than an immediate winding up would secure, or failing that, to realise property so as to make a distribution to creditors.

(b) Appointing an administrator involves sending a notice in the prescribed form identifying the proposed administrator and a statutory declaration that:

    (i)   The company is, or is likely to be, unable to pay its debts

    (ii)   The company is not in liquidation

    (iii) As far as ascertainable there is no restriction in making the appointment

(c) The problem with Lazy Days Ltd's case is whether or not the purpose of administration will be achieved. The company is currently running at a £7,000 loss per month and this must be solvable for the administration order to be granted. If the company can argue that it has a good chance of increasing trip sales from 50% to nearer 80% to 90% and that these extra sales will make up the shortfall in revenue then it would have a good chance of obtaining the order.

27.4

> **Text reference**. Chapter 21.
>
> **Top tips**. This question should be given some thought before you start to write down your answer. It would be a good idea to list the company's debts and the assets it has.

(a) On liquidation Mat, Mary and Norm will be required to contribute the amount unpaid on their shares. Each will have to pay £750 to the company (1,000 × 75p) and this will raise a total of £2,250.

(b) Company assets:

Land valued at £20,000

Other assets £10,000 (£7,750 plus £2,250 raised from the shareholders)

Company's liabilities:

Secured loan £20,000

Business creditors £10,000

Bank overdraft £10,000

The sale of the land will be used to repay the secured loan and this will leave assets of £10,000 to pay creditors of £20,000. The business creditors and the bank will therefore receive half their money back. This would leave the business creditors and the bank owed £5,000 each.

27.5

> **Text reference**. Chapter 21.
>
> **Top tips**. This question is not just about insolvency but also has elements of share capital, borrowing and company charges too. Some syllabus areas are interlinked in this way so you should be prepared to encounter such questions in the exam.

(a)   Earl will become a preferential creditor in respect of his unpaid wages and as such he will only have a claim to have the debt paid to him after the secured creditors have been repaid in full.

(b)   Earl's shares are fully paid. This means the company has received their full nominal value from Earl and he has no further liability in respect of them.

(c)   Earl's debentures are secured by a fixed charge on the land that the factory is built on and he is therefore a secured creditor of the company. Should the company fail to repay the loan or any interest due, the debentureholders may appoint a receiver for the asset who will sell it to realise cash to repay them. As the company is being liquidated the asset will be sold anyway.

28 Fraudulent and criminal behaviour

28.1   A   An insider is a person who has information from an inside source through being a director, employee, shareholder, or because of their employment, office or profession. Customers and suppliers are not likely to be privy to inside information.

Syllabus area H1(a)

28.2   A   Market abuse is a civil law offence.

Syllabus area H1(b)

28.3   C   The initial disposal of the proceeds of a crime is known as placement.

Syllabus area H1(c)

28.4   A   Layering involves the transfer of monies to disguise their original source.

Syllabus area H1(c)

28.5   C   Bribery is a criminal offence. It can occur inside or outside the UK and corporations can be liable if they fail to prevent bribery.

Syllabus area H1(d)

28.6   B   Companies formed by directors of insolvent companies in order to continue their business illegally are known as phoenix companies.

Syllabus area H1(e)

28.7   C   Fraudulent trading under the Insolvency Act 1986 is a civil – not a criminal offence. Any directors found guilty are liable to make good the company's debts.

Syllabus area H1(f)

28.8   A   No expectation of profit is a valid defence to a charge of insider dealing. The other options are not valid defences.

Syllabus area H1(a)

28.9   B   Market abuse involves the deliberate manipulation of the stock market or those trading in the stock market. The issue of a deliberately deceptive profit forecast misleads the market about the company's prospects and is considered market abuse.

Syllabus area H1(b)

28.10   B   The three offences related to money laundering are laundering, failure to report and tipping off.

Syllabus area H1(c)

28.11   A   Suspicions of money laundering should be reported to the National Crime Agency.

Syllabus area H1(c)

28.12   B   Reasonable hospitality is not bribery. Being bribed is an offence under the Act. Non-financial rewards are as much a bribe as the offer of cash. The Act extends around the globe and applies to all

companies registered in the UK. It is also an offence for a corporation to fail to prevent an employee committing bribery.

Syllabus area H1(d)

28.13 B   Intent must be proved in order to win a case of fraudulent trading.

Syllabus area H1(e)

28.14 C   Wrongful trading is a civil offence that is brought by a company's liquidator. No intent to defraud is required because the directors commit the offence if they allow the company to trade whilst in the knowledge that there is no reasonable prospect of the company avoiding going into liquidation.

Syllabus area H1(f)

28.15 A   Wrongful trading is committed when the directors allow a company to trade when there is no reasonable prospect of the company avoiding liquidation. Making a false declaration of solvency is committed when the company wishes to arrange a members' voluntary winding-up and the directors falsely declare that the company is solvent.

Syllabus area H1(f)

29 MTQ Bank 7

29.1

Text reference. Chapter 22.

Top tips. Insider dealing questions tend to encompass more than one of the offences being committed, and this is no exception. While Slye's guilt is very clear, you have to look a little harder to decide on Mate and Tim.

(a)   Slye has inside information as an insider as a director and employee of Huge plc. Slye knows that the information is inside information. He then buys shares in Large plc, which constitutes dealing because he is 'acquiring securities'. He has therefore dealt in price-affected securities while in possession of inside information as an insider, and has committed the offence of insider dealing.

(b)   Mate has knowingly received inside information from a person whom he knows to be an insider (Slye), so he has become an insider and in dealing he too has committed the primary offence of insider dealing.

(c)   Tim did not receive inside information, this is because the information that Slye told him was neither precise nor specific, so he has committed no offence.

29.2

Text reference. Chapter 22.

Top tips. Application of the rules on fraudulent and wrongful trading should not pose you any problems providing you know them. Remember intention must be proved in fraudulent trading cases. In wrongful trading cases liability will be established if it is proved that the defendant knew or should have known about the impending insolvency – directors are deemed to know or should know about the financial position of their company.

(a)   Under s213 Insolvency Act 1986, the offence of fraudulent trading is only actionable if the company is in liquidation. Under s993 Companies Act 2006, the offence is actionable whether or not the company is insolvent.

(b)   (i)   Because Del falsified the company's accounts, and the company is insolvent, he is likely to be guilty of intention to defraud under s213 Insolvency Act 1986. There is not enough evidence to prove Rod is guilty – the prosecution is unlikely to be able to prove he intended to defraud the creditors or others.

        (ii)   Del will be personally liable under s214 Insolvency Act 1986 for the increase in the company's debts since it is already established that he is likely to be liable for fraudulent trading which carries a higher burden of proof. Rod will also be liable for the company's debts, since as a director of a company, he should have been aware of the situation.

29.3

Text reference. Chapter 22.

Top tips. Even if you did not learn the detail about money laundering offences, a feel for what is right or wrong should lead you to the answer. Don't forget that Ian, as an accountant, has a duty to report suspicions of money laundering.

(a) Money laundering is the term given to attempts to make the proceeds of crime appear respectable. It covers any activity by which the apparent source and ownership of money representing the proceeds of crime are changed so that the money appears to have been obtained legitimately.

(b) Ian has assisted in Jet's money laundering, so may be convicted of money laundering under the Proceeds of Crime Act. He may also be found guilty of failure to report under the Proceeds of Crime Act.

(c) Jet is guilty of the main offence of money laundering under the Proceeds of Crime Act.

29.4

Text reference. Chapter 22.

Top tips. There are some areas of the syllabus that you just have to learn and be able to repeat in an exam. The rules on insider dealing are one of them. Make sure you understand the offences.

(a) Vic sold his shares willingly and it is unfortunate for him that the share price subsequently may have risen. He has no right of action.

(b) Under the Criminal Justice Act 1993, Sid is an insider by virtue of his position as director in Trend plc and Umber plc. The information he holds is price-sensitive as it concerns large profits and large losses. Therefore, it would appear that he is liable under for dealing in price-affected securities. None of the defences would apply to him as he clearly expected to make a profit in one transaction and to avoid a loss in the other.

He also becomes liable for the offence of encouraging another to deal in price-affected securities when he advises his brother to buy shares in Umber plc. This is even though we are not told whether the brother actually brought the shares and that no inside information was passed. Sid's offence is merely for encouraging.

29.5

Text reference. Chapter 22.

Top tips. The key to part (c) is remembering that because insider dealing is a criminal offence, the offender may be guilty of money laundering when they dispose of the illegal funds.

(a) Price sensitive means that if the information is made public, it is likely to have a significant effect on share price.

(b) Greg's position as a director of Huge plc makes him an insider, the takeover information is clearly inside information and by instructing Jet Ltd to buy Kop plc shares he was involved in dealing. Therefore he has committed the offence of insider dealing.

(c) The profit on the sale of the Kop plc shares was created as a result of insider dealing – a criminal offence. Greg has sought to disguise the profit by transferring it as a consultancy fee to Imp Ltd and as a dividend to himself. Therefore he has also committed the offence of money laundering.

Mock exams

ACCA Fundamentals Level

Paper F4 ENG

Corporate and Business Law

Mock Examination 1

Question Paper	
Time allowed	**2 hours**
This paper is divided into two sections:	
Section A ALL 45 questions are compulsory and MUST be attempted	
Section B ALL 5 questions are compulsory and MUST be attempted	

Please note that it is not possible to predict question topics in an examination of this nature. We have based the content of this Mock Exam on our long experience of the ACCA exams. We do not claim to have any endorsement of the question types or topics from either the examiner or the ACCA and we do not guarantee that either the specific questions or the general areas that are featured here will necessarily be included in the exams, in part or in whole.

We do not accept any liability or responsibility to any person who takes, or does not take, any action based (either in whole or in part and either directly or indirectly) upon any statement or omission made in this book. We encourage students to study all topics in the ACCA syllabus and this Mock Exam is intended as an aid to revision only.

DO NOT OPEN THIS PAPER UNTIL YOU ARE READY TO START UNDER EXAMINATION CONDITIONS

Section A – ALL 45 questions are compulsory and MUST be attempted

1   In which of the following courts do all criminal cases begin?

    A   County Court
    B   Magistrate's Court
    C   Crown Court   **(1 mark)**

2   Joan holds 100 shares in Box Ltd. The directors of Box Ltd have announced that she will be granted one share for every five shares that she holds. The shares will be issued fully paid-up.

    What is the name given to such an allotment of shares?

    A   Rights issue
    B   Bonus issue
    C   Capital issue
    D   Special issue   **(2 marks)**

3   In the context of sources of law, what is a statutory instrument?

    A   A tool used by Parliament in the process of developing primary legislation
    B   A form of delegated legislation that allows ministerial powers to be exercised
    C   A right granted by the Human Rights Act 1998 to strike out secondary legislation   **(1 mark)**

4   Which of the following is an indication that a person is self-employed rather than an employee?

    A   The person has the ability to delegate work to others
    B   The person is paid a salary
    C   The person is told how they should perform their job
    D   The person has their work tools provided to them   **(2 marks)**

5   Which of the following is a condition that must be met in order for a principal to ratify the actions of an agent?

    A   Ratification must occur immediately after the contract is formed
    B   Ratification must be agreed with the third party
    C   The principal must have existed when the contract was formed   **(1 mark)**

6   What is the minimum notice period that a person who has been employed for eighteen months is entitled to?

    A   One week
    B   One month
    C   Two months   **(1 mark)**

7   In the event of an unlimited liability partnership being terminated, which of the following liabilities are repaid next, once all external debts have been settled?

    A   Partners' loan advances
    B   Partners' capital contributions
    C   Partners' share of profit   **(1 mark)**

8   A declaration of solvency is required to commence which of the following?

    A   A members' voluntary liquidation
    B   A creditors' voluntary liquidation
    C   A compulsory liquidation
    D   An administration   **(2 marks)**

9   A director of a public company may be disqualified if they are absent from board meetings without permission for a particular period of time.

According to the model articles of a public company and as a minimum, after how many months of such absence will a director be disqualified?

A   Two months
B   Three months
C   Six months
D   Twelve months   **(2 marks)**

10 Which of the following companies qualify for exemption from audit?

A   A public company with turnover of £1 million and a balance sheet total of £2 million
B   A private company with turnover of £7 million and a balance sheet total of £5 million
C   A dormant company   **(1 mark)**

11 How many days' holiday leave (including bank holidays) is an employee entitled to as a minimum?

A   21 days
B   25 days
C   28 days   **(1 mark)**

12 Lia was recently dismissed from employment when her employer found out she was pregnant.

Which of the following types of dismissal is this an example of?

A   Constructive dismissal
B   Wrongful dismissal
C   Unfair dismissal   **(1 mark)**

13 In the context of contract law, what is the effect of a counter-offer on the original offer?

A   Acceptance of the original offer as it stands
B   Acceptance of the original offer with new terms introduced
C   Rejection of the original offer
D   No effect on the original offer   **(2 marks)**

14 Holding companies may give creditors of their subsidiary companies a 'letter of comfort' regarding the ability of the subsidiary to pay its debts.

What is the legal effect of a 'letter of comfort'?

A   It is legally binding on the holding company only
B   It is legally binding on the subsidiary company only
C   It is legally binding on the holding company and subsidiary company
D   It is not legally binding on the holding company or subsidiary company   **(2 marks)**

15 In relation to the tort of negligence, which of the following describes the standard of care expected of individuals?

A   What can be reasonably expected of them personally in the circumstances
B   What a reasonable person would do in the circumstances
C   What the person is actually capable of in the circumstances
D   What it is actually possible to do in the circumstances   **(2 marks)**

16 What is the effect of volenti non fit injuria in the law of tort?

A   It is a complete defence to an action in negligence
B   It reduces the amount of damages that a defendant is liable for
C   It reverses the burden of proof so that the defendant must prove that they were not negligent
                                                                                           (1 mark)

17   Bankruptcy cases are heard by which division of the High Court?

    A   Queen's Bench Division
    B   Family Division
    C   Chancery Division   **(1 mark)**

18   In relation to the general rules of statutory interpretation, which of the following is the rule that states 'to express one thing is by implication to exclude anything else'?

    A   Expressio unius est exclusio alterus
    B   Noscitur a socis
    C   In pari materia   **(1 mark)**

19   Which of the following contracts will the Unfair Terms in Consumer Contracts Regulations 1999 apply to?

    A   The supply of commercial goods from one business to another
    B   A contract made in relation to family law
    C   A mobile phone contract from a telecommunications company to a private individual
    D   An employment contract   **(2 marks)**

20   In negligence, what is the limit of a defendant's liability for damages?

    A   The full losses incurred by the claimant
    B   The losses that the defendant could reasonably foresee
    C   The amount of losses that the defendant can afford to pay   **(1 mark)**

21   Which of the following parties does a company auditor owe their duty of care to?

    A   The members personally
    B   The directors
    C   The creditors
    D   The company as a whole.   **(2 marks)**

22   Terms may be implied into a contract of employment if they have certain characteristics.

    Which of the following if a characteristic of a term that may be implied into an employment contract?

    A   The term must be acceptable
    B   The term must be proportionate
    C   The term must be practical
    D   The term must be notorious   **(2 marks)**

23   Which of the following is a lawful excuse for not performing contractual obligations?

    A   The cost of performance has increased from when the contract was formed
    B   Performance is made more difficult due to unforeseen circumstances
    C   The other party has made performance impossible   **(1 mark)**

24   Certain contracts may be made orally but are not enforceable unless they are evidenced in writing.

    Which of the following contracts must be evidenced in writing?

    A   A lease for more than three years
    B   A conveyance
    C   A contract of guarantee
    D   A promise not supported by consideration   **(2 marks)**

25   In a company with more than one member, what is the quorum for a class meeting?

    A   Two persons who hold at least a third of the nominal value of the shares in the class
    B   Three persons who hold at least a half of the nominal value of the shares in the class
    C   Five persons who hold at least a three-quarters of the nominal value of the shares in the class   **(1 mark)**

26   Where a compulsory liquidation order has been granted, which of the following is true?

     A   An insolvency practitioner is appointed as liquidator
     B   All employees are automatically dismissed
     C   Any legal proceedings against the company that are in progress at the time of the liquidation order are allowed to continue
     D   The company's directors continue to run the company whilst the liquidation process is on-going

(2 marks)

27   Which of the following is a rule for valid consideration?

     A   Consideration must pass from the promisor
     B   Consideration must be adequate but not necessarily sufficient
     C   Performance of the promise must be possible
     D   The promise must be given in writing

(2 marks)

28   Which of the following is the final court of appeal for a number Commonwealth countries?

     A   The Supreme Court
     B   The Court of Appeal
     C   The Privy Council

(1 mark)

29   Which of the following is a right of the holder of a debenture that is secured by a fixed charge?

     A   Payment of a company dividend
     B   To vote at the company's general meeting
     C   To vote on company resolutions that affect them as a debentureholder
     D   To prevent the company from selling the asset secured by the charge

(2 marks)

30   In a contract for the sale of goods, an exclusion clause in relation to which of the following terms is automatically void in both consumer and non-consumer contracts?

     A   Title
     B   Description
     C   Sample

(1 mark)

31   Which of the following statements concerning the impact of the Human Rights Act 1998 is NOT correct?

     A   Legislation created before the Act must be interpreted in a manner that is compatible with the European Convention on Human rights
     B   Legislation created after the Act must accompanied with a statement of compatibility with the European Convention on Human Rights
     C   Common law created before the Act must be interpreted in line with decisions of the European Court of Human Rights
     D   The courts may strike out primary legislation that is incompatible with the Act

(2 marks)

32   Liam was convicted of a criminal offence by a Magistrate's Court.

    If Liam has grounds to appeal, which court will the case move to next?

     A   Crown Court
     B   High Court
     C   Court of Appeal
     D   Supreme Court

(2 marks)

33   Which of the following describes the liability of a sole trader for the debts of the business?

     A   Unlimited liability
     B   Limited by the amount they guarantee to pay on winding-up
     C   Limited by the amount of capital in the business

(1 mark)

34   The latest accounts of Tsar Ltd showed that the company had profits available for distribution of £10,000. Mick (the sole director of Tsar Ltd) negligently misinterpreted the accounts and authorised a dividend payment of £20,000. Joan, Mick's wife and shareholder of Tsar Ltd, saw the accounts and knew the dividend was unlawful. The other shareholders did not see the accounts.

Which of the following parties are liable for the unlawful dividend?

    A   Mick only
    B   Joan only
    C   Mick and Joan only
    D   Mick, Joan and all the other shareholders   **(2 marks)**

---

35   An administrator of a company has a number of powers that may or may not require the permission of the court to exercise.

Which of the following is a power that usually requires court approval to exercise?

    A   Appoint a director
    B   Call a meeting of members
    C   Make a payment to a preferential creditor
    D   Make a payment to an unsecured creditor   **(2 marks)**

---

36   LT is an accountant who works for Tapa Ltd, a company owned by SP. LT has devised a scheme where Tapa Ltd can illegally disguise certain revenues so that the company's tax charge is reduced. Any tax that the scheme saves is paid to SP as a dividend.

Which TWO offences has LT committed?

    (1)   Tipping off
    (2)   Failure to prevent
    (3)   Laundering
    (4)   Failure to report

    A   1 and 2
    B   1 and 4
    C   2 and 3
    D   3 and 4   **(2 marks)**

---

37   Ian has recently become a father for the first time.

Which TWO of the following are statutory rights that Ian's employer owes him?

    (1)   The right to statutory paternity leave and pay for a maximum of 2 weeks
    (2)   The right to a change in his terms of employment to allow flexible working
    (3)   The right to unpaid paternity leave for up to 13 weeks per year until the child is age 5
    (4)   The right to protection from redundancy until the child's first birthday

    A   1 and 3
    B   1 and 4
    C   2 and 3
    D   2 and 4   **(2 marks)**

---

38   Which of the following will the Registrar of Companies hold on a company's file?

    A   Copies of all ordinary resolutions
    B   Certificate of incorporation
    C   Minutes from board meetings   **(1 mark)**

---

39   Which of the following reasons is an automatically fair reason for dismissal?

    A   Pregnancy of an employee
    B   The taking part in unofficial industrial action by an employee
    C   Capability of an employee   **(1 mark)**

40   Which TWO of the following are elements of a company's constitution?

(1)   Memorandum of association
(2)   Articles of association
(3)   Company resolutions
(4)   Register of members

A   1 and 2
B   1 and 4
C   2 and 3
D   3 and 4   **(2 marks)**

41   Which TWO of the following are criminal offences that directors of a company may commit as a consequence of their company being insolvent?

(1)   Acting as a director whilst disqualified
(2)   Making a false declaration of solvency
(3)   Wrongful trading
(4)   Abuse of position

A   1 and 2
B   1 and 4
C   2 and 3
D   3 and 4   **(2 marks)**

42   Which of the following remedies for breach of contract involves the injured party claiming the value of the work they have done?

A   Quantum meruit
B   Action for the price
C   Specific performance
D   Rescission   **(2 marks)**

43   In relation to contract law, which of the following statements in relation to acceptance of an offer is correct?

A   Acceptance may be indicated by a person's silence
B   Acceptance must be made verbally
C   Acceptance may be inferred from a person's actions   **(1 mark)**

44   Which of the following parties are owed a duty of care by an accountant in respect of accounts that they have produced?

A   The client only
B   The client and any person relying on the accounts
C   The client and any person that the accountant knows will rely on the accounts
D   The client and to the public at large   **(2 marks)**

45   In which TWO of the following contracts will intention to create legal relations be presumed?

(1)   A contract between a man and his brother in relation to the transfer of property between them
(2)   A contract between two friends for one to wash the other's car
(3)   A contract between a mother and daughter for the daughter to pay the mother housekeeping money while she lives at home
(4)   A contract of employment between a company and an employee

A   1 and 2
B   1 and 4
C   2 and 3
D   3 and 4   **(2 marks)**

Section B – ALL 5 questions are compulsory and MUST be attempted

1   Adam, who operates an accountancy practice, charges £1,000 per year for producing business accounts for tax purposes. Unfortunately he has had some difficulty in recovering his fees from two clients as follows.

Bob, a car mechanic, told Adam that he could only raise cash to pay half of his fees but that he would service Adam's car for the coming year. Adam reluctantly agreed to this proposal.

Dawn, a not very successful musician, also told Adam that she could only pay half the money she owed him as she needed to use the other half to finance her new recording. Once again Adam agreed to accept the half payment. Dawn's recording subsequently became a major hit and she made £100,000 profit from it.

Adam himself is now in financial difficulty and needs cash to pay his own tax bill.

Required

(a)	Explain whether Adam can require Bob to pay his fees in full.	**(2 marks)**
(b)	Explain the effect of promissory estoppel on Dawn's payment to Adam.	**(2 marks)**
(c)	Explain how Adam may be able to obtain full payment from Dawn.	**(2 marks)**
		(Total = 6 marks)

2   Chi, Di and Fi formed an ordinary partnership to run an art gallery. Each of them paid £100,000 into the business. As Fi had no prospect of raising any more money it was agreed between them that her maximum liability for any partnership debts would be fixed at her original contribution of £100,000. The partnership agreement specifically restricted the scope of the partnership business to the sale of 'paintings, sculptures and other works of art.' In January 20X0 Chi took £10,000 from the partnership's bank drawn on its overdraft facility. She had told the bank that the money was to finance a short-term partnership debt but in fact she used the money to pay for a holiday. In February Di entered into a £25,000 contract on behalf of the partnership to buy some books, which she hoped to sell in the gallery.

Required

(a)	State whether all three partners are liable to repay the overdraft created by Chi	**(2 marks)**
(b)	State the type of authority Di had to purchase the books.	**(2 marks)**
(b)	State the liability of Fi for the partnership's debts.	**(2 marks)**
		(Total = 6 marks)

3   In 20X0 Fay, Gus and Het formed a private limited company, FGH Ltd, to carry out technological research. They each took 100 shares in the company and each of them became a director in the company.

In January 20X2 Fay admitted that she had been working with a much larger rival company, Ix plc, and that she had passed on some of FGH Ltd's research results to Ix plc in return for substantial payment. Fay maintains that she has done no harm, as FGH Ltd was not capable of using the information. Nonetheless, Gus and Het are extremely angered by Fay's actions.

Required

(a)	Explain the consequences to directors who are in breach of their duties to their company.	
		(2 marks)
(b)	State the duties to FGH Ltd that Fay has breached.	**(2 marks)**
(c)	Explain how Gus and Het may remove Fay from being a director of FGH Ltd.	**(2 marks)**
		(Total = 6 marks)

4   Two years ago Fin inherited some money and decided to invest the money in company shares.

At that time he heard that Heave Ltd was badly in need of additional capital and that the directors had decided that the only way to raise the needed money was to offer fully paid up £1 shares to new members at a discount price of 50p per share. Fin thought the offer was too good to miss and he subscribed and paid for 20,000 new shares on this basis. However, Heave Ltd has since gone into insolvent liquidation, owing a considerable sum of money to its unsecured creditors.

With the remaining money of his investment Fin subscribed for 10,000 shares in Irk plc. Although they were nominally £1 shares, he was required to pay a premium of £1 for each share he subscribed for. The shares are currently trading at £2 per share.

Required

(a)   Explain the extent of Fin's liability for Heave Ltd's debts.   **(2 marks)**

(b)   Explain

   (i)   The purpose of a share premium account

   (ii)   Whether Fin can reclaim his premium payment from Irk plc   **(4 marks)**

                                                                       (Total = 6 marks)

5   Jaz plc is listed on the London Stock Exchange. Kip works for Jaz plc as an accountant. Whilst drawing up the annual accounts, Kip noticed that Jaz plc's profits were better than anyone could have expected. As a consequence of this knowledge, he bought shares in Jaz plc before its good results were announced. He made a substantial profit on the share dealing. Kip also told his friend Lu about the results before they were announced. Lu also bought shares in Jaz plc.

Required

(a)   State the definition of inside information.   **(2 marks)**

(b)   Explain whether Kip and Lu have committed the offence of insider dealing.   **(4 marks)**

                                                                       (Total = 6 marks)

Answers

DO NOT TURN THIS PAGE UNTIL YOU HAVE
COMPLETED THE MOCK EXAM

SECTION A

1   B   All criminal cases begin in a Magistrate's Court with the more serious cases moving to the Crown Court afterwards. County Courts are in the civil court system and mainly deal with contract and tort cases.

Syllabus area A1(b)

2   B   The allotment of additional, fully paid-up shares, in proportion to the holding of each shareholder is a bonus issue. A rights issue requires the shareholder to pay for the extra shares issued.

Syllabus area E1(c)

3   B   A statutory instrument is a form of delegated legislation that allows ministerial powers to be exercised.

Syllabus area A2(b)

4   A   The ability to delegate work is an indication of self-employment. The other options are indications that the person is employed.

Syllabus area C1(a)

5   C   To ratify the contract, the principal must have existed when it was formed and ratification must take place within a reasonable period of time. Ratification must be communicated to the third party, but their agreement to the ratification is not required.

Syllabus area D1(b)

6   A   If a person is employed between one month and two years they are entitled to one week's notice.

Syllabus area C2(a)

7   A   After external debts have been settled, loan advances from partners are repaid next followed by partners' capital contributions and then any profits are shared out.

Syllabus area D2(e)

8   A   A declaration of solvency is required to commence a members' voluntary liquidation. It is not required in the other options.

Syllabus area G1(a)

9   B   Three months of absence without permission is sufficient to disqualify a director of a public company.

Syllabus area F1(b)

10   C   Dormant companies are exempt from audit. Public companies are never exempt from audit. Private companies are exempt from audit if they have turnover of less that £6.5 million and a balance sheet total of less than £3.26 million.

Syllabus area F2(b)

11   C   Every employee is entitled to a minimum of 28 days' holiday leave.

Syllabus area C1(b)

12   C   Dismissal on the grounds of pregnancy is an automatically unfair reason for dismissal. Wrongful dismissal occurs when insufficient notice is given to an employee. Constructive dismissal occurs when the employer repudiates an essential term of the employment contract and the employee resigns.

Syllabus area C2(d)

13   C   A counter-offer has the effect of rejecting the original offer.

Syllabus area B1(c)

14   D   A 'letter of comfort' is not legally binding on the holding company or subsidiary company.

Syllabus area B1(h)

15   B   The standard of care is what a reasonable person would do in the circumstances.

Syllabus area B4(c)

16   A   *Volenti non fit injuria* is a complete defence to an action in negligence. The defendant is not liable because the claimant voluntarily accepted the risk of injury or loss. Contributory negligence reduces the amount of damages that a defendant must pay. *Res ipsa loquitur* reverses the burden of proof.

Syllabus area B4(e)

17   C   Bankruptcy cases are heard by the Chancery Division. The Queen's Bench Division mainly deals with contract and tort cases. The Family Division deals with family related cases.

Syllabus area A1(b)

18   A   *Expressio unius est exclusio alterus* means to express one thing is by implication to exclude anything else. *Noscitur a socis* means that it is presumed that words draw meaning from those around them. In *pari materia* means if the statute forms part of a series that are on a similar subject, the court may look to the interpretation of previous statutes on the assumption that Parliament intended the same thing.

Syllabus area A2(c)

19   C   UTCCR 1999 only applies to consumer contracts. The other options are examples of contracts that are excluded from the scope of the regulations.

Syllabus area B2(c)

20   B   A claimant is only liable for the losses that they could reasonably foresee and this may mean that the defendant does not receive damages in respect of all the losses suffered.

Syllabus area B4(d)

21   D   Since the *Caparo* case, auditors only owe a duty of care to the company as a whole.

Syllabus area C1(b)

22   D   Terms may be implied into contracts from custom and practice if they are reasonable, certain and notorious.

Syllabus area A1(b)

23   C   A party will have a lawful excuse not to perform their obligations if the other party has made performance impossible. An increase in cost is not a lawful excuse, nor is performance being more difficult.

Syllabus area B3(a)

24   C   A contract of guarantee must be evidenced in writing. The other options are contracts that must be made by deed.

Syllabus area B1(a)

25   A   The quorum for a class meeting is 2 members who hold at least a third of the nominal value of the shares in the class.

Syllabus area F3(c)

26   B   Once a liquidation order has been granted all employees are automatically dismissed. The official receiver is appointed as liquidator and runs the company during the liquidation process. Existing legal proceedings are halted and new proceedings may not commence.

Syllabus area G1(b)

27	C	To be valid consideration, the promise must be possible. It must pass from the promise. Consideration must be sufficient but not necessarily adequate. It does not have to be given in writing.

Syllabus area B1(e)

28	C	The Judicial Committee of the Privy Council is the final court of appeal for a number of Commonwealth countries. It's decisions have a persuasive influence over points of law in the English legal system.

Syllabus area A1(b)

29	D	Debentureholders do not have the right to dividends, to attend company meetings or to vote on company resolutions. However, if the debenture is secured by a fixed charge, they may prevent the company from selling the asset that the charge is secured on.

Syllabus area E2(b)

30	A	Terms relating to title may not be subject to an exclusion clause in either consumer or non-consumer contracts. The other options are void in a consumer contract but subject to a reasonableness test in a non-consumer contract.

Syllabus area A1(b)

31	D	All legislation must be interpreted in a manner that is compatible with the Convention. New legislation must be accompanied with a statement of compatibility. Common law must be interpreted in line with decisions of the European Court of Human Rights. The courts may strike out secondary, not primary, legislation.

Syllabus area A2(d)

32	B	Appeals from a Magistrate's Court are heard by the High Court (Queen's Bench Division).

Syllabus area A1(b)

33	A	A sole trader has unlimited liability for the debts of the business.

Syllabus area D3(a)

34	C	Directors who misinterpret the accounts will be liable for an unlawful dividend. Relief may be granted if the mistake was honest and reasonable, but this is not the case here because the misinterpretation was due to negligence. Only shareholders who know the dividend was unlawful are liable.

Syllabus area D3(b)

35	D	An administrator usually requires court approval to make payments to unsecured creditors. The other actions do not require court approval.

Syllabus area G1(e)

36	D	LT has assisted SP in laundering money from a criminal offence (tax evasion) and is also liable for failing to report SP's money laundering activities.

Syllabus area H1(c)

37	A	A new father is entitled to 2 weeks' of paternity leave and pay after the birth of his child. He is also entitled to 13 weeks' of unpaid parental leave per year until the child is aged 5. He has the right to apply for flexible working, but it does not have to be granted. There is no protection from redundancy available.

Syllabus area C1(b)

38	B	As well as sending a certificate of incorporation to the company, the Registrar will keep a copy on the company's file. Not all ordinary resolutions will be filed. Copies of board minutes are not sent to the Registrar.

Syllabus area D4(d)

| 39 | B | Taking part in unofficial industrial action and being a threat to national security are the two automatically fair reasons for dismissal. Pregnancy is an automatically unfair reason. Capability is a potentially fair reason. |

Syllabus area C2(d)

| 40 | C | A company's constitution consists of its articles of association and any resolutions or agreements that it makes. |

Syllabus area D4(e)

| 41 | C | All the offences may be committed by directors, but only making a false declaration of solvency and wrongful trading are a consequence of insolvency – ie they can only be committed by directors of insolvent companies. |

Syllabus area A1(b)

| 42 | A | In a *quantum meruit* claim, the injured party claims the value of the work done. An action for the price is an action to recover a specific amount, usually the price of goods supplied. Specific performance involves the defendant performing the contract as agreed. Rescission involves reversing what has happened so all parties are returned to the pre-contract status quo. |

Syllabus area B3(c)

| 43 | C | Acceptance may be inferred by a person's actions. It cannot be indicated by a person's silence but does not have to be made verbally either. |

Syllabus area B1(d)

| 44 | C | An accountant owes a duty of care to those they have a special relationship with. This includes the client that the accounts were prepared for, but also to anyone who the accountant knows will rely on the accounts. |

Syllabus area B4(f)

| 45 | B | The courts will infer intention where property is transferred between family members. An employment contract is commercial in nature and therefore intention is presumed. The other options are domestic matters where intention is not presumed. |

Syllabus area B1(h)

SECTION B

1

(a) Adam agreed to accept Bob's servicing of his car as a payment in kind. He may not recover any further sum from Bob *(Anon 1495)*. Consideration need not be 'adequate' at law but must be sufficient so the question of whether servicing of the car is valuable enough is not relevant.

(b) *Prima facie*, Adam's agreement to accept only half of the debt appears to be unsupported by consideration and therefore Adam may still claim the remaining amount. However, Dawn may claim he cannot do so because of the doctrine of promissory estoppel, since she acted on the strength of his waiver by spending the remaining debt money on her recording.

(c) If Adam can show that he did not accept part payment voluntarily or that Dawn took advantage of his financial difficulty, he may be entitled to recover following *D and C Builders v Rees 1966*. Alternatively, it may be argued that following the success of Dawn's recording, her reliance on the waiver was not to her detriment and it would be inequitable to allow her to avoid her obligations. The circumstances are such that it may be just to allow Adam to enforce his legal rights *(Combe v Combe 1951)*.

2

(a) Chi has taken money from the firm's bank account to use for a personal holiday. However, as a partner, and in the absence of any specific mention to the contrary in the agreement, she has authority to withdraw money from the bank account. Her action has therefore incurred a debt to a third party that is owed by all three partners, not just herself.

(b) The partnership agreement specifies that the partnership should only sell paintings, sculptures and other works of art, so Di did not have actual authority to undertake this contract. However, the third party is not privy to the partnership agreement so is not aware that the contract is beyond the scope of the partnership. Therefore, Di has apparent authority to undertake the contract on behalf of the other partners.

(c) Because both the overdraft and contract for the books are binding on the partnership all three partners are personally liable if the partnership does not have sufficient funds to pay them. Fi is jointly liable for the debts of the partnership to the third parties. However as the partnership agreement limits her liability to £100,000 she will be able to claim any amount over this from Chi and Di.

3

(a) Consequences for directors that are in breach of their duties include:

- Damages payable to the company where it has suffered loss
- Restoration of company property
- Repayment of any profits made by the director
- Rescission of contract (where the director did not disclose an interest)

(b) Under the Companies Act 2006, Fay is in breach of her s175 duty to avoid conflict of duty and personal interest. This is because she did not disclose her interest in Ix plc and she obtained a personal advantage through this interest. She is also in breach of her s176 duty not to accept benefits from third parties when she accepted the substantial payment from Ix plc for passing on information.

(c) Gus and Het could seek Fay's removal as a director of FGH Ltd. To do this they would have to provide the company with special (28 day) notice to arrange a general meeting. They would then need to arrange for an ordinary resolution to be voted on at the meeting, calling for her removal. They have sufficient numbers of shares between them to meet the requirements of a simple majority.

4

> **Text reference.** Chapters 15 and 17.
>
> **Top tips.** Read a question like this at least twice and make certain that you have fully absorbed all of the information in it before you put pen to paper.

(a) On allotment, it is possible for part of the payment for shares to be deferred to a future date. In such cases the shares are referred to as 'partly paid'. In the event of the shares being transferred, the unpaid capital passes with the shares as a debt payable by the holder at the time when payment becomes due. Fin is therefore liable to Heave Ltd for the unpaid element of 50p per share. He will therefore have to pay up to a maximum of £10,000 to Heave Ltd, depending on the actual liabilities of the company.

(b) (i) A company may issue shares for a price in excess of the nominal value of those shares. The excess is called the 'share premium' and must be credited to a share premium account. The general rule is that reduction of the share premium account is subject to the same restrictions as reduction of share capital. No part of the account can be distributed as dividend. The account can be used to pay up fully paid shares under a bonus issue since this operation simply converts one form of fixed capital into another. It can also be used to pay issue expenses and commissions in respect of a new share issue.

   (ii) Applying the above to the present scenario, it is apparent that Irk plc cannot repay in cash any amount of the share premium account to Fin or any other shareholders.

5

> **Text reference.** Chapter 22.
>
> **Top tips.** There are some areas of the syllabus that you just have to learn and be able to repeat in an exam. The rules on insider dealing are one of them. Make sure you understand this offence.

(a) The Criminal Justice Act 1993 defines inside information as information:

- Relating to particular securities
- Being specific or precise
- Not made public
- Likely to have a significant effect on the price of securities

(b) Kip is an insider by virtue of his position as an accountant in Jaz plc. The information he holds is price-sensitive because it concerns large profits. Therefore, it would appear that he is liable under for dealing in price-affected securities. None of the defences would apply to him as he clearly expected to make a profit.

He also becomes liable for the offence of encouraging another to deal in price-affected securities when he advises Lu to buy shares in Jaz plc.

Lu received inside information from Kip who he knew to be an insider. Therefore he is liable, like Kip, for trading using inside information.

ACCA Fundamentals Level

Paper F4 ENG

Corporate and Business Law

Mock Examination 2

Question Paper	
Time allowed	**2 hours**
This paper is divided into two sections: Section A ALL 45 questions are compulsory and MUST be attempted Section B ALL 5 questions are compulsory and MUST be attempted	

Please note that it is not possible to predict question topics in an examination of this nature. We have based the content of this Mock Exam on our long experience of the ACCA exams. We do not claim to have any endorsement of the question types or topics from either the examiner or the ACCA and we do not guarantee that either the specific questions or the general areas that are featured here will necessarily be included in the exams, in part or in whole.

We do not accept any liability or responsibility to any person who takes, or does not take, any action based (either in whole or in part and either directly or indirectly) upon any statement or omission made in this book. We encourage students to study all topics in the ACCA syllabus and this Mock Exam is intended as an aid to revision only.

DO NOT OPEN THIS PAPER UNTIL YOU ARE READY TO START UNDER EXAMINATION CONDITIONS

BPP LEARNING MEDIA

Section A – ALL 45 questions are compulsory and MUST be attempted

1   In a case that is being heard under the civil law, which of the following is the injured party?

    A   The prosecution
    B   The claimant
    C   The defendant   **(1 mark)**

2   What is a treasury share?

    A   A share issued on terms that it may be brought back by the company at a future date
    B   A share offered to members to purchase pro rata to their existing holding
    C   A share given fully-paid to existing members
    D   A share created when a company purchases its own shares for cash or out of distributable profit   **(2 marks)**

3   Which rule of statutory interpretation means that words in an Act should be given their grammatical meaning?

    A   The literal rule
    B   The golden rule
    C   The mischief rule   **(1 mark)**

4   Which of the following is an example of wrongful dismissal?

    A   Dismissal with insufficient notice
    B   Dismissal on grounds of trade union membership
    C   The repudiation of an essential term of the employment contract by the employer resulting in the resignation of the employee
    D   Dismissal on grounds of pregnancy   **(2 marks)**

5   Hamble is the Chief Executive Officer of Bead Ltd. In a communication with one of Bead Ltd's suppliers, Hamble states that Avery is now an agent of Bead Ltd and that the supplier should in future communicate with Bead Ltd through Avery.

    Which type of agency agreement has been created?

    A   Agency by estoppel
    B   Agency by necessity
    C   Agency by implied agreement   **(1 mark)**

6   An employment contract can be in which of the following forms?

    A   Written only
    B   Oral only
    C   Written or oral   **(1 mark)**

7   Which of the following describes the liability of partners who retire from an unlimited partnership?

    A   Liable for partnership debts only up until the date of retirement
    B   Liable for partnership debts incurred before and after retirement
    C   Liable for partnership debts until all creditors of the firm have been notified of their retirement   **(1 mark)**

8   A liquidation committee is involved in which of the following insolvency procedures?

    A   Members' voluntary liquidation
    B   Creditors's voluntary liquidation
    C   Compulsory liquidation
    D   Administration   **(2 marks)**

9   George is a director of two companies that operate in the same industry, Zip Ltd and Bung Ltd. Both Zip Ltd and Bung Ltd have recently tendered for the same contract with Jane Ltd. Only one company will be awarded the contract.

    Which statutory duty of a director is George in breach of?

    A   Act within powers
    B   Exercise independent judgement
    C   Not to accept benefits from third parties
    D   Avoid conflicts of interest   **(2 marks)**

10 Which of the following is NOT a test used by the courts to determine the employment status of an employee?

    A   Control test
    B   Integration test
    C   Delegation test   **(1 mark)**

11 Which of the following is a legitimate method for an auditor to leave office?

    A   Written resolution with a 75% majority
    B   Ordinary resolution with 14 days' notice of the meeting
    C   Resignation of the auditor before the end of their term of office   **(1 mark)**

12 Which of the following is a remedy for unfair dismissal?

    A   Re-engagement as an employee of the employer
    B   Damages for breach of employment contract
    C   Damages for the employer's negligence   **(1 mark)**

13 Which of the following is NOT an essential element of a valid contract?

    A   Acceptance
    B   Invitation to treat
    C   Intention to create legal relations
    D   Consideration   **(2 marks)**

14 Which of the following is the name given to something that induces the formation of a contract but does not become a term of the contract?

    A   Condition
    B   Warranty
    C   Representation
    D   Statement   **(2 marks)**

15 In relation to the tort of negligence, what is novus actus interveniens?

    A   A decision by the court that reverses the burden of proof
    B   An intervening act that may break the chain of causality
    C   An event that makes the damage too remote so that the defendant is not liable
    D   A defence to a liability in negligence   **(2 marks)**

16   Which type of legal wrong is 'passing-off' classified as?

    A   A criminal offence
    B   A breach of contract
    C   A tort   **(1 mark)**

17   The Queen's Bench Division is a part of which of the following courts?

    A   The Court of Appeal
    B   The Supreme Court
    C   The High Court   **(1 mark)**

18   In the English civil law system, the decision of which of the following courts may be appealed directly to the Supreme Court?

    A   Crown Court
    B   County Court
    C   High Court   **(1 mark)**

19   Gup has a contract to supply Jud with a computer on 31 March 20X1. On 2 March 20X1 Gup tells Jud that due to demand in the market for computer chips, the cost of supplying the computer has increased and that he will no longer be able to supply it.

    On 2 March 20X1, which of the following options is available to Jud?

    A   Jud may treat the contract as discharged, but cannot sue for damages until after 31 March
    B   Jud must allow the contract to continue until actual breach occurs and then sue for damages
    C   Jud may treat the contract as discharged and sue for damages on 2 March, or allow the contract to continue until actual breach occurs and then sue for damages
    D   Jud must accept that Gup's performance is impossible and there is no legal remedy for him

                    (2 marks)

20   In which of the following circumstances does volenti non fit injuria apply?

    A   Where the claimant accepted the risk of loss or damage
    B   Where the claimant fully or partly contributed to their losses
    C   Where the claimant accepts the burden of proof   **(1 mark)**

21   DDD plc requested a meeting with the auditor of a company that it wanted to takeover in order to discuss the company's finances. In the meeting, the senior partner of audit firm stated that the target company's latest accounts can be relied upon. The takeover took place and it was discovered that the accounts of the target company understated debts by £10 million.

    Which of the following describes the legal position of the audit firm?

    A   The auditor does not owe a duty of care to DDD plc because it was not a client of the firm
    B   The auditor does not owe a duty of care to DDD plc because the accounts are not intended as advice in a takeover
    C   The auditor owes DDD plc a duty of care because of the statement of the senior partner
    D   The auditor owes DDD plc a duty of care because they could have foreseen that the accounts may be used in a takeover   **(2 marks)**

22   What is the statutory minimum notice period that an employee with 12 years of service has to give their employer when they wish to terminate their employment?

    A   1 week
    B   4 weeks
    C   6 weeks
    D   12 weeks   **(2 marks)**

23   Which type of consideration has been provided where goods are delivered and payment is made at the same time?

    A   Executory consideration
    B   Executed consideration
    C   Past consideration   **(1 mark)**

24   Luce sent an email to Brice that asked 'Will you sell your car to me?'. Brice sent an email in reply that stated 'The price of the car is £2,000'.

How will Brice's email to Luce be treated under contract law?

    A   As an offer
    B   As an invitation to treat
    C   As a supply of information
    D   As an invitation to tender   **(2 marks)**

25   In relation to company meetings, what is a proxy?

    A   A person appointed by a shareholder to attend the meeting and vote on their behalf
    B   A person who presides over the meeting
    C   A person who counts the votes cast by members on a resolution   **(1 mark)**

26   One ground for a creditor to apply for the compulsory liquidation of a company is that they are owed a minimum amount of money, they have issued a written demand for payment of what is owed and the company fails to repay the debt or offer reasonable security for it within 21 days.

What is the minimum amount of debt owed by the company for this procedure to apply?

    A   £500
    B   £750
    C   £1,000
    D   £1,500   **(2 marks)**

27   Which of the following statements concerning consideration is correct?

    A   Consideration must be adequate
    B   Consideration must be sufficient
    C   Consideration from each party must be of equal value
    D   Consideration must be present in all contracts   **(2 marks)**

28   Which of the following types of right under the Human Rights Act 1998 is subject to restriction in order to take the public interest into account?

    A   Absolute rights
    B   Qualified rights
    C   Derogable rights   **(1 mark)**

29   Which of the following will NOT cause a floating charge to crystallise?

    A   Liquidation of the company
    B   Sale of the assets the charge is secured on
    C   Cessation of the company's business
    D   Appointment of a receiver by the chargee   **(2 marks)**

30   Which of the following is the remedy to the injured party in the event of a breach of warranty?

    A   Treat the contract as discharged only
    B   Claim damages only
    C   Treat the contract as discharged and claim damages   **(1 mark)**

31 The Criminal Division of the Court of Appeal normally hears appeals from which of the following courts?

    A   High Court
    B   Crown Court
    C   County Court
    D   Magistrate's Court   **(2 marks)**

---

32 In the context of the English legal system, what are 'Rules of Court'?

    A   A form of delegated legislation
    B   Parliamentary procedures followed in the formation of primary legislation
    C   A handbook used by Judges when interpreting primary legislation
    D   Guidance given to Judges when applying the Human Rights Act 1998   **(2 marks)**

---

33 A private limited company is distinguished from other corporate forms by what at the end of its name?

    A   plc
    B   Ltd
    C   LLP   **(1 mark)**

---

34 In relation to the payment of dividends, which of the following is a distributable reserve?

    A   Capital redemption reserve
    B   Revaluation reserve
    C   Retained earnings
    D   Share premium account   **(2 marks)**

---

35 Which of the following will prevent a company from appointing an administrator?

    A   The company is currently unable to pay its debts
    B   A resolution of the floating chargeholders with a 75% majority
    C   A receiver currently in office at the company
    D   A declaration of solvency from the directors   **(2 marks)**

---

36 In relation to insider dealing, information that is 'made public' is not classed as inside information.

Which of the following is information that is 'made public'?

    (1)   Information that is published under the rules of the regulated market
    (2)   Information concerning public companies
    (3)   Information communicated by the company Chairman
    (4)   Information published in The Gazette

    A   1 and 2
    B   1 and 4
    C   2 and 3
    D   3 and 4   **(2 marks)**

---

37 Which TWO of the following must be included on an employee's statement of prescribed particulars given to them soon after they commence employment?

    (1)   Job title
    (2)   Entitlement to flexible working
    (3)   Provision of training facilities
    (4)   Details of pensions or pension schemes

    A   1 and 2
    B   1 and 4
    C   2 and 3
    D   3 and 4   **(2 marks)**

38   Which party is NOT liable on a pre-incorporation contract?

    A   The company
    B   The third party
    C   The promoter   **(1 mark)**

39   After what period of continuous service does an employee become eligible for redundancy pay?

    A   12 months
    B   18 months
    C   24 months   **(1 mark)**

40   Which TWO of the following parties are bound by a company's constitution?

    (1)   The company's shareholders
    (2)   The company's suppliers
    (3)   The company's debentureholders
    (4)   The company itself

    A   1 and 2
    B   1 and 4
    C   2 and 3
    D   3 and 4   **(2 marks)**

41   Which TWO of the following are valid defences available to a charge of bribery?

    (1)   The person did not expect to make a profit
    (2)   The person was exercising their function as a member of the intelligence service
    (3)   The person was exercising their function as a member of the armed forces on active service
    (4)   The person had reasonable grounds for their conduct

    A   1 and 2
    B   1 and 4
    C   2 and 3
    D   3 and 4   **(2 marks)**

42   Which of the following is NOT a type of repudiatory breach of contract?

    A   Renunciation
    B   Incapacitation
    C   Frustration
    D   Breach of condition   **(2 marks)**

43   How is an advertisement of goods for sale treated under contract law?

    A   As an offer
    B   As a supply of information
    C   As an invitation to treat   **(1 mark)**

44   In the tort of negligence what is the effect of the 'egg-shell skull' rule?

    A   The claimant is expected to take extra care if they are more prone to injury
    B   The claimant is expected to have notified the defendant that they are at a high risk of injury
    C   The defendant is expected to take the victim as they find them
    D   The defendant is expected to assume liability for unforeseeable damage to the claimant if the claimant is especially vulnerable   **(2 marks)**

45   Terms of a contract may include exclusion clauses limiting a party's liability for losses due to negligence.

Which TWO of the following exclusion clauses are only valid if reasonable?

(1)   Liability for death
(2)   Liability for economic loss
(3)   Liability for damage to a vehicle
(4)   Liability for personal injury

A   1 and 2
B   1 and 4
C   2 and 3
D   3 and 4

(2 marks)

SECTION B – ALL 5 questions are compulsory and MUST be attempted

1   Ali is a dealer in Persian rugs and placed an advertisement in his local paper stating: 'Once in a lifetime opportunity to own a handmade Persian antique rug for only £1,500 – cash only. This is a serious offer – the rug will go to the first person who accepts it – offer valid for one day only – today Saturday'.

When Bud saw the advert, he immediately posted a letter of acceptance of Ali's offer in order to make sure he got the rug. Cil also saw the advert and after inspecting the rug offered Ali a cheque for £1,500, but he refused to accept the cheque and told her she could not have the rug. Later in the day, Das asked Ali if he would keep the offer open until he could get to his bank to arrange a loan. Ali agreed, but subsequently, when Ed offered to pay £2,000 in cash for the rug, Ali sold the rug to him.

On Monday morning Bud's letter arrived, and Das returned to complete his purchase of the rug.

Required

(a)   Explain whether Bud has entered into a binding contract with Ali   **(2 marks)**
(b)   Explain whether Cil has entered into a binding contract with Ali   **(2 marks)**
(c)   Explain whether Das has any right of action against Ali   **(2 marks)**

(Total = 6 marks)

---

2   Brian is the manager of a distribution warehouse that supplies a number of Do-It-Yourself stores. Following the introduction of a new computerised stock record system, Brian is dismissed, because he is unable to adapt to the new working practices – no warnings were given and no disciplinary action was taken before his dismissal. Brian has worked for the company for fifteen years. As a result of the re-organisation, John is also dismissed because of his involvement in trade union activities. He has worked for the company for nine months.

Brian is seeking compensation for redundancy and John intends to make a claim for unfair dismissal.

Required

(a)   Identify the remedies for unfair dismissal   **(2 marks)**
(b)   State whether Brian will be successful in claiming redundancy compensation   **(2 marks)**
(c)   State whether John will be successful in a claiming unfair dismissal   **(2 marks)**

(Total = 6 marks)

---

3   Mat is in the process of setting up an IT business as a private limited company. He has been told that in order to register the company he should submit appropriate articles of association and a memorandum of association.

He also thinks that because there is an existing similar, local business called Netscape Ltd it would be a good idea to call his new company Netscope Ltd based on the chance that he could transfer some of its business to his new company.

Required

(a)   State the purpose of a company's articles of association and memorandum of association.

(2 marks)

(b)   Explain

(i)   What is meant by 'passing-off' in relation to company names
(ii)   Whether the owners of Netscape Ltd could take a passing-off action against Mat if he decides to name his business Netscope Ltd   **(4 marks)**

(Total = 6 marks)

4   Five years ago Kim, Liz and Meg formed Orb Ltd in which Kim and Liz each hold 40% of the shares and Meg owns the remaining 20%. They are the only directors. The objects of Orb Ltd contained in its articles are restricted to research, production and marketing environmentally-friendly cleaning products.

In the course of a research project for Orb Ltd, Kim discovered a new highly powerful industrial cleaner, but unfortunately it is extremely toxic and not at all environmentally-friendly. She persuaded Liz that Orb Ltd should sell the new product and the pair recently signed a contract with Zeeb Ltd to distribute it.

Meg maintains that the contract is contrary to the restrictions stated in Orb Ltd's articles and is not binding on the company.

Required

(a)   State the legal capacity of a registered company to contract   **(2 marks)**
(b)   Explain
       (i)   Whether Zeeb Ltd may enforce its contract with Orb Ltd
       (ii)   Whether Meg may stop Kim and Loz marketing the new product   **(4 marks)**

                                                                                   (Total = 6 marks)

5   Martha is the finance director of a publicly listed chain of fashion stores. The company is finding it increasingly hard to pay its creditors as its sales are falling rapidly and the point has been reached where Martha must decide whether to close the failing business down or to battle on, even though the business is unlikely to pull through.

Em jointly owns a rival store. It too is experiencing financial difficulties and she is thinking about starting a members' voluntary winding up to close the company down.

Required

(a)   State the criminal offence Em may commit if a members' voluntary winding up is commenced
                                                                                              (2 marks)

(b)   Explain any liability Martha may have in relation to:
       (i)   Fraudulent trading under s213 Insolvency Act 1986
       (ii)   Wrongful trading under s214 Insolvency Act 1986   **(4 marks)**

                                                                                   (Total = 6 marks)

Answers

**DO NOT TURN THIS PAGE UNTIL YOU HAVE
COMPLETED THE MOCK EXAM**

SECTION A

1   B   In the civil law system the injured party is known as the claimant and the person who the case is being brought against is known as the defendant. The prosecution is the party bringing a case under the criminal law.

Syllabus area A1(a)

2   D   A treasury share is created when a company buys its own shares for cash or out of distributable profit. A redeemable shares is issued on the basis that the company can buy it back at a future date. A rights issue is where shares are offered to members to buy pro rata to their existing holding. A bonus issue is where shares are given fully-paid to the existing members.

Syllabus area E1(b)

3   A   The literal rule states that words should be given their grammatical meaning. The golden rule states that the literal rule should be followed unless it could give an absurd result. The mischief rule states that the judge should consider what mischief the Act was intended to prevent.

Syllabus area A2(c)

4   A   Wrongful dismissal is dismissal with insufficient notice. Dismissal on grounds of trade union membership or pregnancy is unfair dismissal. The repudiation of an essential term of the employment contract by the employer that results in the resignation of the employee is constructive dismissal.

Syllabus area C2(c)

5   A   Hamble is 'holding out' to the supplier that Avery is an agent of Bead Ltd. Therefore an agency by estoppel has been created.

Syllabus area D1(b)

6   C   An employment contract can be in written or oral form.

Syllabus area C1(b)

7   C   Retiring partners are liable for partnership debts, incurred before and after the retirement until all creditors are notified of their retirement.

Syllabus area D2(d)

8   B   A liquidation committee is involved in a creditors' voluntary liquidation.

Syllabus area G1(a)

9   D   George has a conflict of interest because both companies want to win the contract, but only one will be successful. The interests of both companies are in conflict.

Syllabus area F1(d)

10   C   The three tests used by the courts to determine employment status are the control test, integration test and multiple (economic reality) test.

Syllabus area C1(a)

11   C   An auditor may resign from office during their term by giving the company notice in writing. They cannot be removed by a written resolution, but can be removed with an ordinary resolution with special (28 day) notice of the meeting.

Syllabus area F2(b)

12   A   The three remedies for unfair dismissal are reinstatement (same employer, same job), re-engagement (same employer, different job), or compensation (based on a statutory calculation not breach of contract).

Syllabus area A1(b)

| 13 | B | The essential elements of a valid contract are offer, acceptance, intention to create legal relations and consideration. |
| | | Syllabus area B1(a) |

| 14 | C | A representation is something that induces a contract but does not become a term of the contract. Conditions and warranties are types of contractual term. A statement may be a term or a representation. |
| | | Syllabus area B2(a) |

| 15 | B | Novus actus interveniens are intervening acts, such as by the claimant or a third party, that may break the chain of causality. |
| | | Syllabus area B4(d) |

| 16 | C | 'Passing-off' is a type of tort. |
| | | Syllabus area B4(b) |

| 17 | C | The Queen's Bench Division is a divisional court of the High Court. |
| | | Syllabus area A1(b) |

| 18 | C | In the civil law system, appeals to the Supreme Court are usually made from the Court of Appeal (not listed as an option). However, an appeal can also be made from the High Court via the leapfrog procedure. |
| | | Syllabus area A1(b) |

| 19 | C | Gup's performance is not impossible, just more expensive, and therefore he has committed anticipatory breach of contract. In this situation, Jud is entitled to treat the contract as discharged and sue for damages immediately, or allow the contract to continue and sue for damages at that point. |
| | | Syllabus area B3(b) |

| 20 | A | *Volenti non fit injuria* is a defence to a liability in negligence and applies if the claimant voluntarily accepted the risk of injury or loss. |
| | | Syllabus area B4(e) |

| 21 | C | In general, an auditor does not owe a duty of care to the public, shareholders and others who buy or increase their stake in a company due to the *Caparo* decision. However, the statement by the senior partner is sufficient to create a duty of care because the firm knew that the accounts would be relied upon in a takeover. |
| | | Syllabus area B4(f) |

| 22 | A | The statutory minimum notice period of an employee, regardless of length of service, is one week. |
| | | Syllabus area C2(a) |

| 23 | B | Executed consideration occurs at the present time – goods are delivered and the price is paid. Executory consideration is a promise given for a promise – a promise to pay for goods when they are delivered at a future time. Past consideration occurs before the contract is made. |
| | | Syllabus area B1(e) |

| 24 | C | A statement of the price of an item is treated as a supply of information, *Harvey v Facey 1893*. |
| | | Syllabus area A1(b) |

| 25 | A | A proxy is a person appointed by a shareholder to attend the meeting and vote on their behalf. It is the chairman that presides over the meeting. |
| | | Syllabus area F3(c) |

| 26 | B | The creditor must be owed at least £750 for the procedure to apply. |
| | | Syllabus area G1(b) |

| 27 | B | Consideration must be sufficient but need not be adequate. Consideration does not need to be of equal value. Contracts that are in the form of a deed do not require consideration. |

Syllabus area B1(f)

| 28 | B | Qualified rights are subject to restriction in order to take the public interest into account. The Government may opt out of derogable rights but not simply for reasons of public interest. Absolute rights cannot be restricted in any circumstances. |

Syllabus area A2(d)

| 29 | B | Sale of the assets that the charge is secured on does not cause the charge to crystallise. The other options all cause the charge to crystallise. |

Syllabus area E2(d)

| 30 | B | Damages are the only remedy where a warranty is breached. Breach of a condition allows the injured party to treat the contract as discharged and claim damages. |

Syllabus area B2(b)

| 31 | B | The Criminal Division of the Court of Appeal hears appeals from the Crown Court. |

Syllabus area A1(b)

| 32 | A | Rules of Court are a form of delegated legislation that allow the judiciary to control court procedure. |

Syllabus area A2(b)

| 33 | B | A private limited company is identified by Ltd at the end of its name. A public limited company has plc and a limited liability partnership has LLP. |

Syllabus area D3(a)

| 34 | C | Distributable reserves include reserves of realised profits less realised losses, for example retained earnings. The other options are all none distributable reserves. |

Syllabus area E3(b)

| 35 | C | A company may not appoint an administrator if a receiver is already in office. Being unable to pay its debts is a ground for appointing an administrator. |

Syllabus area G1(e)

| 36 | B | The key word in the two correct answers is 'published'. Information published under rules of the regulated market and contained in public records, such as *The Gazette*, are public information. The other options have not been made public and could have been disclosed privately. |

Syllabus area H1(a)

| 37 | B | Job title and details of pensions or pensions schemes are included on the statement. The other options are not. |

Syllabus area C1(b)

| 38 | A | The company is not liable on a pre-incorporation contract because it did not exist when the contract was formed. The parties to the contract are the promoter and the third party. |

Syllabus area D4(b)

| 39 | C | An employee must have two years of continuous service to be eligible for redundancy pay. |

Syllabus area C2(f)

| 40 | B | A company's constitution only binds the company and its members (the shareholders). |

Syllabus area D4(e)

| 41 | C | Only members of the armed forces or intelligence service that are properly exercising their function have a defence to bribery charges. |

Syllabus area H1(d)

42   C   Frustration is a lawful excuse for failure to perform contractual obligations. The other options are types of repudiatory breach of contract.

Syllabus area B3(b)

43   C   An advertisement of goods for sale is treated as an invitation to treat.

Syllabus area B1(b)

44   C   The 'egg-shell skull' rule states that the defendant is expected to take the victim as they find them.

Syllabus area B4(c)

45   C   Clauses that limit liability for death or personal injury are void. Clauses relating to other types of loss or damage must be reasonable.

Syllabus area A1(b)

SECTION B

1

(a) Ali's advert stated that the offer is for Saturday only (the day the advert was displayed) and therefore it is fair to say that the use of the post is outside his contemplation and so postal rule does not apply. Bud has no contract with Ali because his attempt to accept the offer uses an unacceptable method.

(b) Cil made an offer to buy the rug from Ali for the asking price, but by cheque rather than cash. Ali did not accept the cheque. By introducing new terms (payment by cheque not cash) Cil made a counter-offer to Ali. Ali rejected this offer and therefore there is no contract between them.

(c) Das requested some extra time to arrange a bank loan to buy the rug and Ali agreed. This agreement was revoked by Ali when he sold the rug to Ed. If it is found that Das had a separate option contract with Ali to hold the offer open for him then Das would have an action against Ali for breach of contract. Das would have to prove that he gave something by way of consideration for Ali holding the offer open and it is possible that a court would find taking out a bank loan is valid consideration in this case.

2

(a) Remedies for unfair dismissal include, reinstatement (ie a return to the same job without any break in the continuity of employment), re-engagement (which is a different but comparable job with the same employer) and compensation (consisting of a basic award, calculated on age, length of service and weekly wage). There may also be a compensatory award for additional losses calculated on ordinary principles of breach of contract which should represent the amount which the tribunal considers to be just and equitable in all the circumstances.

(b) Brian has been dismissed because he has been unable to adapt to new works practices, not by reason of redundancy. Redundancy occurs where a person's skills are no longer required by the employer, for example where the business is relocated, closes down or is liquidated. Brian is not entitled to claim redundancy compensation.

(c) John has been dismissed because of his involvement in trade union activities and has worked for the company for nine months. Under the Act, a dismissal is automatically unfair (regardless of length of service) if it is on account of an employee's trade union membership or activities. Therefore John has a valid claim.

3

(a) A company's articles of association is part of its constitution that deals with matters affecting the internal conduct of the company's affairs including the issue and transfer of shares and class rights, dividends and alterations of capital structure, the convening and conduct of general meetings, the appointment, powers and proceedings of directors and company accounts. The memorandum is a document that is signed and dated by the subscribers of the company. It states that the subscribers wish to form a company and that they undertake to subscribe for at least one share.

(b)　(i)　At common law, a company can be prevented from using a name if the use of that name causes the company's goods to be confused with those of another company. The court may grant an injunction in a passing off action brought by that other company and may also force the defendant company to change its name. For example, in *Ewing v Buttercup Margarine Co Ltd 1917* a sole trader was prevented from using the business name 'The Buttercup Dairy Co' in the north of England because of confusion with the business in the London area of Buttercup Margarine Co Ltd.

(ii)　Mat is likely to be liable for an action in passing-off, particularly because of the similarity in business types and their location near each other. The case against him is strengthened because he declared that his aim is to benefit from the goodwill of an existing company. He is advised not to call his new company Netscope Ltd.

4

> **Text reference**. Chapter 14.
>
> **Top tips**. You must be very well-prepared to be able to earn good marks on the ultra vires doctrine. Ensure you are familiar with the law in this area and spend a few moments thinking about your answer before starting to write.

(a)　The contractual capacity of a registered company is usually unrestricted and it may enter into any lawful contract. However the members may resolve to restrict the activities of the company (the objects), or the articles may have included restrictions at the time the company was registered.

(b)　(i)　Any contract entered into that is affected by such restrictions is known as ultra vires, and in theory it is void. However, given that the validity of a company's acts cannot be questioned on the grounds of it having lacked legal capacity (under s39 of the Companies Act 2006), the ultra vires rule is of very limited effect insofar as third parties are concerned. Therefore Zeeb Ltd may enforce its contract with Orb Ltd.

(ii)　Due to the impact of s39 of the Companies Act 2006, Meg will not be able to prevent Orb Ltd from being bound by its contract with Zeeb Ltd. Her colleagues may well seek to unrestrict the company's objects by special resolution which, since they control 80% of the shares, would be successful. Therefore Meg cannot stop her fellow directors from marketing the product.

5

> **Text reference**. Chapter 22.
>
> **Top tips**. Do not confuse fraudulent and wrongful trading. Remember the key difference is that intention to defraud must be proved in fraudulent trading cases.

(a)　When companies go into a members' voluntary winding up, the directors must make a declaration of solvency – ie a declaration that the company is not insolvent. It is a criminal offence to make such a declaration without having reasonable grounds to do so. Therefore Em must be certain that the business is solvent before commencing the members' voluntary winding up or she risks committing this offence.

(b)　(i)　Fraudulent trading occurs when a company intended to defraud its creditors. If it is proved in respect of a company that has gone into liquidation, the persons who decide to carry on trading may become liable for the company's debts. On the evidence provided, it is unlikely that Martha will be found guilty of this offence, as it does not appear that she intends to defraud the creditors of the company.

(ii)　The offence of wrongful trading was introduced because it is often difficult to prove intention in fraudulent trading cases. Under this offence, the directors of a company become liable for its debts if they continue to trade even if they knew or should have known that there was no reasonable prospect of the company avoiding going into liquidation. The test is whether or not a reasonably diligent person with the general knowledge, skill and experience that might be reasonably expected of a person carrying out the particular director's duties would have continued to trade. From the evidence, it appears that the company is unlikely to pull through, therefore Martha risks committing wrongful trading if she decides to continue to trade.

ACCA Fundamentals Level

Paper F4 ENG

Corporate and Business Law

Mock Examination 3

Specimen Paper

Question Paper	
Time allowed	2 hours
This paper is divided into two sections:	

This paper is divided into two sections:

Section A   ALL 45 questions are compulsory and MUST be attempted

Section B   ALL 5 questions are compulsory and MUST be attempted

DO NOT OPEN THIS PAPER UNTIL YOU ARE READY TO START UNDER EXAMINATION CONDITIONS

SECTION A – ALL 45 questions are compulsory and MUST be attempted

1   Which of the following may imply terms into contracts?

    A   Statute
    B   Third parties
    C   The parties to the contract   **(1 mark)**

2   There are a number of ways in which investors can take an interest in a company and such different interests have different rights attached to them.

    Which of the following NORMALLY participate in surplus capital?

    A   Preference shares
    B   Ordinary shares
    C   Debentures secured by a fixed charge
    D   Debentures secured by a floating charge   **(2 marks)**

3   In the context of the English legal system, which of the following courts ONLY has civil jurisdiction?

    A   Magistrates' court
    B   County court
    C   High Court   **(1 mark)**

4   In the context of employment law, which of the following is an AUTOMATICALLY fair ground for dismissing an employee?

    A   Unofficial industrial action
    B   Redundancy
    C   Refusal to join a trade union
    D   Legal prohibition   **(2 marks)**

5   Which of the following business forms does the use of the abbreviation 'Ltd' after the name of a business indicate?

    A   A limited partnership
    B   A limited liability partnership
    C   A private limited company   **(1 mark)**

6   Jas has been continuously employed for six years.

    Which of the following states the minimum period of notice she is entitled to?

    A   One month
    B   Six weeks
    C   Three months   **(1 mark)**

7   Which of the following is indicated by the abbreviation 'Ltd' at the end of a company's name?

    A   The shares are not transferable
    B   The shares may not be offered to the public
    C   The shares are freely transferable on the stock exchange   **(1 mark)**

8   Section 122 Insolvency Act 1986 specifically provides a distinct ground for applying to have a company wound up on the ground that it is just and equitable to do so.

Which of the following parties may petition to have a company compulsorily wound up under that provision?

    A   Shareholders of the company
    B   Creditors of the company
    C   Debentureholders of the company
    D   The Secretary of State   **(2 marks)**

9   Mo has a significant holding in the shares of Nova Ltd. He wishes to use his shareholding to remove Owen from the board of directors but is not sure how to do so.

Which of the following must be used to remove a director from office?

    A   An ordinary resolution
    B   An ordinary resolution with special notice
    C   A special resolution
    D   A written resolution   **(2 marks)**

10   A written ordinary resolution requires the approval of which of the following?

    A   More than 50% of those actually voting
    B   More than 50% of those entitled to vote
    C   Unanimous approval of those entitled to vote   **(1 mark)**

11   Employment law is a mixture of common law and statutory provisions.

Which of the following is purely based on statute law?

    A   Summary dismissal
    B   Unfair dismissal
    C   Wrongful dismissal   **(1 mark)**

12   Jo's contract of employment states that she is employed in Glasgow. When her employer tells her that she has to work in London, some 500 miles away, Jo immediately resigns.

Which of the following may this be considered an example of?

    A   Unfair dismissal
    B   Constructive dismissal
    C   Summary dismissal   **(1 mark)**

13   Which parties are bound by the terms of the tender when one party submits a tender?

    A   The person submitting the tender
    B   The person requesting the tender
    C   Both parties
    D   Neither party   **(2 marks)**

14   In the context of contract law, a bid at an auction is which of the following?

    A   An invitation to treat
    B   An offer
    C   A counter-offer
    D   An acceptance   **(2 marks)**

15 Bee injured her eye after failing to close a safety gate on a machine as instructed. She was also not wearing mandatory safety goggles as required by her contract of employment.

Which of the following is this an example of?

A   Novus actus interveniens
B   Volenti non fit injuria
C   Res ipsa loquitur
D   Contributory negligence   **(2 marks)**

16 What is the effect of a finding of contributory negligence in the law of tort?

A   It removes the requirement to pay damages
B   It reverses the payment of damages
C   It decreases the level of damages   **(1 mark)**

17 In the context of the English legal system, which of the following courts ONLY has criminal jurisdiction?

A   A Magistrates' Court
B   The Crown Court
C   A County Court   **(1 mark)**

18 Imran claims that Zak owes him £1,000 as a result of a breach of contract.

In which court will Imran start his action against Zak?

A   A Magistrates' Court
B   A County Court
C   The High Court   **(1 mark)**

19 In the context of case law, which of the following applies to an obiter dictum?

A   It is binding on all future courts
B   It is binding on all lower courts
C   It is not binding on any courts
D   It is not binding outside the court it was issued in   **(2 marks)**

20 Contributory negligence arises as a result of the fault of which of the following?

A   The claimant
B   The respondent
C   A third party   **(1 mark)**

21 Ann got trapped in a public toilet due to the lock being faulty. Rather than wait for help, she tried to climb out of the window but fell and broke her leg.

Which of the following is this an example of?

A   Res ipsa loquitur
B   Volenti non fit injuria
C   Novus actus interveniens
D   Contributory negligence   **(2 marks)**

22 The law treats employees differently from the self-employed and has established a number of tests to distinguish between the two categories.

Which of the following is NOT a test for establishing an employment relationship?

A   The subordinate test
B   The control test
C   The integration test
D   The economic reality test   **(2 marks)**

23 Breach of which of the following terms does NOT allow the possibility of the aggrieved party terminating the contract?

    A   A condition
    B   A warranty
    C   An innominate term   **(1 mark)**

24 Which of the following, in the context of entering into a contract, constitutes a binding offer to sell a unique item of furniture?

    A   Placing an advert in a newspaper with a price attached
    B   Placing it on display inside a shop with a price attached
    C   Telling someone the price you may be willing to accept for it
    D   Telling someone you will reduce the marked price on it by 10%   **(2 marks)**

25 Mark has received the agenda for the annual general meeting of Rova Ltd, a company he has shares in. The agenda contains a number of resolutions to be proposed at the meeting, but being a new member Mark is not certain as to what is exactly involved.

In the context of company meetings, which of the following must be passed by a 75% majority to be effective?

    A   An ordinary resolution with special notice
    B   A special resolution
    C   A written resolution   **(1 mark)**

26 Section 122 Insolvency Act 1986 provides a number of distinct grounds for applying to have a company wound up on a compulsory basis.

Which of the following is NOT a ground for the compulsory winding up of a company under that provision?

    A   The company has not received a trading certificate within its first 12 months
    B   The company has not started trading within the first 12 months
    C   The company has suspended its business for 12 months
    D   The company has altered its primary business within the first 12 months   **(2 marks)**

27 Abe issued an invitation to tender for a contract and Bea submitted her terms.

Which of the following statements is accurate?

    A   Abe made an offer which Bea accepted
    B   Abe made an invitation to treat and Bea made an offer
    C   Both Abe and Bea made invitations to treat
    D   Abe made an offer and Bea made a counter-offer   **(2 marks)**

28 In the context of statutory interpretation, which of the following requires judges to consider the wrong which the legislation was intended to prevent?

    A   The mischief rule
    B   The literal rule
    C   The golden rule   **(1 mark)**

29 It is not unusual for some company investments to carry cumulative dividend rights.

Which of the following statements about the declaration of cumulative dividends is correct?

    A   They are not paid until profits reach a certain percentage
    B   They are paid in the form of a bonus issue
    C   They are paid out of capital
    D   They are paid when profits are available for that purpose   **(2 marks)**

30   Which of the following statements in relation to effective consideration is correct?

    A   It must be both adequate and sufficient
    B   It must be adequate but need not be sufficient
    C   It must be sufficient but need not be adequate   **(1 mark)**

---

31   In the context of the English legal system, which of the following defines the ratio decidendi of a judgement?

    A   The decision in a previous case
    B   The facts of the case
    C   The legal reason for deciding the case
    D   The future application of the case   **(2 marks)**

---

32   Dan has been accused of a criminal offence and is due to be tried soon. He denies responsibility, claiming that the prosecution has no evidence that he committed the offence in question.

Which of the following describes the standard of proof in a criminal case?

    A   On the balance of probability
    B   On the balance of certainty
    C   Beyond reasonable doubt
    D   Beyond evident doubt   **(2 marks)**

---

33   Which of the following statements relating to limited liability partnerships is correct?

    A   They are limited to a maximum of 20 members
    B   They must have a minimum of two members
    C   They must have at least one unlimited member   **(1 mark)**

---

34   Ho subscribed for some partly paid-up shares in Io Ltd. The company has not been successful and Ho has been told that when Io Ltd is liquidated, he will have to pay the amount remaining unpaid on his shares. However, he is not sure to whom such payment should be made.

In limited liability companies, shareholders are liable to which party for any unpaid capital?

    A   Creditors
    B   The directors
    C   The company
    D   The liquidator   **(2 marks)**

---

35   Which of the following CANNOT petition for the compulsory winding up of a company on the grounds of INSOLVENCY under s.122 Insolvency Act 1986?

    A   The board of directors
    B   The members of the company
    C   The company's creditors
    D   The Secretary of State   **(2 marks)**

---

36   Money laundering involves a number of phases in the overall procedure.

Which TWO of the following are recognised phases in money laundering?

    (1)   Relocation
    (2)   Layering
    (3)   Integration
    (4)   Distribution

    A   1 and 2
    B   1 and 4
    C   2 and 3
    D   3 and 4   **(2 marks)**

37   Which TWO of the following are AUTOMATICALLY unfair grounds for dismissing an employee?

(1)   Engaging in trade union activity
(2)   Constructive dismissal
(3)   Dismissal on transfer of employment to a new undertaking
(4)   Redundancy

A   1 and 2
B   2 and 3
C   3 and 4
D   1 and 3   **(2 marks)**

---

38   In the context of the law of agency, an agent will NOT be liable for a contract in which of the following instances?

A   Where the agent fails to disclose that they are acting as such

B   Where the agent intends to take the benefit of the contract and does not disclose they are acting as an agent

C   Where the agent acts on their own behalf although claiming to be an agent   **(1 mark)**

---

39   The Employment Rights Act (ERA) 1996 sets out remedies in relation to unfair dismissal.

Which of the following is NOT a potential remedy for unfair dismissal under the ERA 1996?

A   Reinstatement
B   Re-engagement
C   Re-employment   **(1 mark)**

---

40   Which TWO statements are correct in relation to designated members in limited liability partnerships (LLPs)?

(1)   They must not take part in the day-to-day operation of the business
(2)   They are responsible for filing the LLP's accounts
(3)   They are fully liable for partnership debts
(4)   They have limited liability

A   1 and 4
B   2 and 4
C   2 and 3
D   1 and 3   **(2 marks)**

---

41   The term insider dealing relates to a number of potential criminal offences.

Which TWO of the following are crimes in relation to insider dealing?

(1)   Encouraging someone to engage in insider dealing
(2)   Failing to report insider dealing
(3)   Concealing insider dealing
(4)   Passing on inside information

A   1 and 2
B   1 and 4
C   2 and 3
D   2 and 4   **(2 marks)**

---

42   Which of the following can be accepted so as to form a binding contract?

A   A supply of information
B   A statement of intent
C   A quotation of price
D   An agreement to enter into a future contract   **(2 marks)**

43   Contracts are legally enforceable agreements.

Which of the following statements regarding contractual agreements is true?

A   They must be in writing
B   They must be evidenced in writing
C   They need not be in writing   **(1 mark)**

44   In relation to the law of negligence, a finding of volenti non fit injuria arises from the action of which of the following?

A   The claimant
B   The respondent
C   A third party
D   An unforeseeable event   **(2 marks)**

45   In the context of the law of contract, which TWO of the following statements in relation to a letter of comfort are correct?

(1)   It is a binding promise to pay a subsidiary company's future debts
(2)   It is a non-binding statement of present intention to pay a subsidiary company's future debts
(3)   It is issued by a parent company
(4)   It is issued by a parent company's bank

A   1 and 3
B   2 and 3
C   2 and 4
D   1 and 2   **(2 marks)**

SECTION B – ALL 5 questions are compulsory and MUST be attempted

1   Az Ltd operates a shipbuilding business which specialises in constructing and modifying ships to order. In 2011, Az Ltd entered into an agreement with Bob to completely rebuild a ship to Bob's specification for a total contract price of £7 million. However, after completion, Bob informed Az Ltd that, due to the downturn in the world economy, he no longer needed the ship. Az Ltd had already expended £5 million on altering the ship, and immediately started an action against Bob for breach of contract.

However, in the week before the case was to be decided in the court, Az Ltd sold the ship for the same amount of money which they would have received from Bob.

Required

(a)	State the purposes of awarding damages for breach of contract	**(2 marks)**
(b)	State the duty to mitigate losses	**(2 marks)**
(c)	State the level of damages Az Ltd can claim for breach of contract	**(2 marks)**

(Total = 6 marks)

---

2   Clare, Dan and Eve formed a partnership 10 years ago, although Clare was a sleeping partner and never had anything to do with running the business. Last year Dan retired from the partnership. Eve has subsequently entered into two large contracts. The first one was with a longstanding customer, Greg, who had dealt with the partnership for some five years. The second contract was with a new customer, Hugh. Both believed that Dan was still a partner in the business. Both contracts have gone badly wrong, leaving the partnership owing £50,000 to both Greg and Hugh. Unfortunately the business assets will only cover the first £50,000 of the debt.

Required

(a)	State the liability of Clare as a sleeping partner	**(2 marks)**
(b)	Identify the liabilities of Dan as a retiring partner	**(2 marks)**
(c)	State from whom Greg can claim the outstanding debt	**(2 marks)**

(Total = 6 marks)

---

3   Jon, who is 65 years of age, has just retired from his employment with a pension and a lump sum payment of £100,000. He is keen to invest his money but has absolutely no knowledge of business or investment. He does not wish to take any great risk with his investment but he would like to have a steady flow of income from it.

He has been advised that he can invest in the following range of securities:

(1)   Preference shares
(2)   Ordinary shares
(3)   Debentures secured by a fixed charge
(4)   Debentures secured by a floating charge

Required

In relation to the above investment forms:

(a)	Identify which is the most secure	**(2 marks)**
(b)	State which may have a cumulative right to dividends	**(2 marks)**
(c)	State which NORMALLY participates in surplus capital	**(2 marks)**

(Total = 6 marks)

4   In 2008 Ger was disqualified from acting as a company director for a period of 10 years under the Company Directors Disqualification Act 1986 for engaging in fraudulent trading.

However, he decided to continue to pursue his fraudulent business and, in order to avoid the consequences of the disqualification order, he arranged for his accountant Kim to run the business on his instructions. Although Kim took no shares in the company, and was never officially appointed as a director, he nonetheless assumed the title of managing director.

Required

(a)   Identify which of the following categories of directors apply to Ger and Kim:

    (i)   De facto
    (ii)   De jure
    (iii)   Non-executive
    (iv)   Shadow   **(4 marks)**

(b)   State the working relationship and duties of non-executive directors   **(2 marks)**

(Total = 6 marks)

---

5   Fran and Gram registered a private limited company, Ire Ltd, in January 2009, with each of them becoming a director of the company.

Although the company did manage to make a small profit in its first year of trading, it was never a great success and in its second year of trading it made a loss of £10,000.

At that time Fran said he thought the company should cease trading and be wound up. Gram, however, was insistent that the company would be profitable in the long term so they agreed to carry on the business, with Fran taking less of a part in the day-to-day management of the company, although retaining his position as a company director.

In the course of the next three years Gram falsified Ire Ltd's accounts to disguise the fact that the company had continued to suffer losses, until it became obvious that he could no longer hide the company's debts and that it would have to go into insolvent liquidation, with debts of £100,000.

Required

(a)   State whether criminal or civil action, or both, can be taken in relation to fraudulent trading and wrongful trading   **(2 marks)**

(b)   Explain whether Fran or Gram will be liable for either of the following:

    (i)   Fraudulent trading under s213 Insolvency Act 1986
    (ii)   Wrongful trading under s214 Insolvency Act 1986   **(4 marks)**

(Total = 6 marks)

Answers

DO NOT TURN THIS PAGE UNTIL YOU HAVE
COMPLETED THE MOCK EXAM

Fundamentals Level – Skills Module, Paper F4 (ENG)
Corporate and Business Law (English)   **Specimen Exam Answers**

SECTION A

1	A
2	B
3	B
4	A
5	C
6	B
7	B
8	A
9	B
10	A
11	B
12	B
13	A
14	B
15	B
16	C
17	B
18	B
19	C
20	A
21	D
22	A
23	B
24	D
25	B
26	D
27	B
28	A
29	D
30	C
31	C
32	C
33	B
34	C
35	B
36	C
37	D
38	A
39	C
40	B
41	B
42	C
43	C
44	A
45	B

SECTION B

1   (a)   Damages in contract are intended to compensate an injured party for any financial loss sustained as a consequence of another party's breach. The object is not to punish the party in breach, so the amount of damages awarded can never be greater than the actual loss suffered. The usual aim of the award of damages is to put the injured party in the same position they would have been in had the contract been properly performed (expectation loss).

    (b)   The duty to mitigate losses ensures that the injured party is under a duty to take all reasonable steps to minimise their loss. As a result, the seller of goods, which are not accepted, has not only to try to sell the goods to someone else but is also required to get as good a price as they can when they sell them *(Payzu v Saunders (1919))*. If goods are not delivered under a contract, the buyer is entitled to go into the market and buy similar goods, paying the market price prevailing at the time. They can then claim the difference in price between what they paid and the original contract price as damages.

    (c)   Applying the foregoing to the contract between Az Ltd and Bob, it can be seen that Az Ltd managed to recoup all of the costs and potential profit it would have made on the contract with Bob, so is not in a position to claim any further damages from Bob.

2   (a)   Her status as a sleeping partner gives Clare no additional protection from the unlimited liability which applies to all ordinary partners in an ordinary partnership. It simply means she has left her personal wealth open to clams over which she has no practical control through her own inaction.

    (b)   He remains liable to existing customers until those customers are informed that he has left the partnership.

          He also remains liable to new customers who knew he was a member of the partnership, unless he has made public his withdrawal.

    (c)   Greg can claim from all three parties: Clare, Dan and Eve.

3   (a)   As loans, debentures are more secure than shares. Debentures secured by fixed charges are more secure than those secured by floating charges. Consequently, debentures secured by fixed charges are the most secure form of investment of those listed. They do, however, receive the least in terms of return.

    (b)   Of the four investment forms only shares receive dividends, as debentures receive interest due to the fact that they are forms of loan. Of the share forms only the preference share can carry a right to a cumulative dividend, as ordinary shares only get a return on the profits generated by the company in any particular year.

    (c)   Only shares have any claim against surplus capital, as debentures are only secured against the amount loaned.

          Of the two types of shares, preference shares MAY have rights to enjoy access to surplus capital but ONLY ordinary shares have such facility as a right.

4   (a)   Ger acts behind the scenes and is clearly operating as a shadow director. Kim has not been appointed as such but acts as a director, which makes him a de facto director.

    (b)   As with all directors, non-executives owe fiduciary duties (now stated in statute) to their company. They are also subject to all legal regulation applying to ordinary directors. They may attend company meetings and have full voting rights.

5   (a)   Criminal liability is only applicable to fraudulent trading under the Companies Act 2006. However, civil action is open under ss213 and 214 Insolvency Act 1986 in relation to both fraudulent and wrongful trading.

    (b)   As a consequence of his falsification of the accounts, Gram is potentially liable under s213 Insolvency Act 1986 fraudulent trading provisions.

          Fran, on the other hand, may not have been liable for fraud but is certainly liable for wrongful trading for not taking the appropriate action to prevent the subsequent losses sustained by the company.

Section A

1–45   One or two marks per question; total marks 70

Section B

1   (a)   1 mark for each relevant point made relating to damages up to the maximum 2 marks.

    (b)   1 mark for each relevant point made relating to the duty to mitigate losses, up to the maximum 2 marks.

    (c)   1 mark for correct application and 1 mark for explanation.

2   (a)   1 mark for each relevant point made relating to the potential liability of Clare as a sleeping partner, up to the maximum 2 marks.

    (b)   1 mark for each relevant point made relating to the potential liability of Dan as a retired partner, up to the maximum 2 marks.

    (c)   Full 2 marks only to be given to a fully correct answer.

          Partial answers to be limited to 1 mark.

3   (a)   1 mark for correct statement and 1 mark for explanation.

    (b)   1 mark for correct statement and 1 mark for explanation of cumulative rights.

    (c)   1 mark for correct statement and 1 mark for explanation of surplus capital.

4   (a)   3–4 marks for a complete explanation of the different types of director and a correct application to Ger and Kim.

          1–2 marks for some understanding but lacking either application or explanation.

          0 marks for no understanding of the substance of the question.

    (b)   1 mark for each relevant point made relating to the role/function of non-executive directors, up to the maximum 2 marks.

5   (a)   A full answer distinguishing between fraudulent and wrongful trading is required for both marks to be given.

          1 mark for any relevant point made relating to either action.

    (b)   4 marks for a full answer clearly distinguishing the two types of activity and correctly applying them.

          1 mark each for correctly stating how each provision will be applied to the parties.

          1 mark for any relevant point made relating to either party's action.

Review Form – Paper F4 Corporate and Business Law (Eng) (06/14)

Name: _____   Address: _____

_____

_____

How have you used this Kit?
(Tick one box only)

☐ Home study (book only)

☐ On a course: college _____

☐ With 'correspondence' package

☐ Other _____

Why did you decide to purchase this Kit?
(Tick one box only)

☐ Have used the complementary Study text

☐ Have used other BPP products in the past

☐ Recommendation by friend/colleague

☐ Recommendation by a lecturer at college

☐ Saw advertising

☐ Other _____

During the past six months do you recall seeing/receiving any of the following?
(Tick as many boxes as are relevant)

☐ Our advertisement in *Student Accountant*

☐ Our advertisement in *Pass*

☐ Our advertisement in *PQ*

☐ Our brochure with a letter through the post

☐ Our website www.bpp.com

Which (if any) aspects of our advertising do you find useful?
(Tick as many boxes as are relevant)

☐ Prices and publication dates of new editions

☐ Information on product content

☐ Facility to order books off-the-page

☐ None of the above

Which BPP products have you used?

Text	☐	Passcards	☐	Home Study Package	☐
Kit	☑	i-Pass	☐		

Your ratings, comments and suggestions would be appreciated on the following areas.

	Very useful	Useful	Not useful
Passing F4 (Eng)			
Questions			
Top Tips etc in answers			
Content and structure of answers			
Mock exam answers			

Overall opinion of this Kit	Excellent	☐	Good	☐	Adequate	☐	Poor ☐

Do you intend to continue using BPP products?   Yes ☐   No ☐

The BPP Learning Media ACCA Range Manager of this edition can be e-mailed at: pippariley@bpp.com

Please return this form to: Pippa Riley, ACCA Range Manager, BPP Learning Media Ltd, FREEPOST, London, W12 8AA

Review Form (continued)

TELL US WHAT YOU THINK

Please note any further comments and suggestions/errors below.